*How Commitment to Excellence, Quality of Care,
and Passion Led to 46 Years of Healthcare Success*

TALLER
THAN THE
TREES

JOHN STEWART

BRIGHTRAY
P U B L I S H I N G ®

We help busy professionals write and publish their stories
to distinguish themselves and their brands.

(407) 287-5700 | Winter Park, FL
info@BrightRay.com | www.BrightRay.com

ISBN: 978-1-956464-51-1

Published in the United States of America.
BrightRay Publishing ® 2024

Working on the Heart Center of Indiana was one of my fondest memories and a career highlight. I will always be grateful for the example John Stewart, Deeni Taylor, Lana Lehman, and Jim Bremner set— that caring for the team around them and driving for excellence can both be achieved together."

—**Ben Rooke**,
Regional President at Brasfield & Gorrie, LLC

The challenge was to design and construct the Heart Center in less than 14 months. With the focus of our team, we accomplished and exceeded all expectations."

—**Deeni Taylor**,
Former Chief Strategy Officer at St. Vincent Health, Head of Strategic Relationships at HealthPeak

This book is dedicated to the transplant team and Storm Eye Institute of the Medical University of South Carolina, in addition to the selfless actions of my donor and his family. Thank you for helping extend my journey.

TABLE OF CONTENTS

FOREWORD

After 40 years as a professional consultant, I have had the distinct pleasure of working with many of the top leaders in the world. I have served in various industries as a consultant to management, an executive coach, a therapist, an author, and a public speaker. Many of the excerpts from my speeches became known as "Lumpkinisms," quotes or nuggets of wisdom that people still remember to this day. One of them is: *"People support that which they help to create."*

My journeys have allowed me to share the paths of many people who excelled in their fields, such as Dr. William Glasser, Dr. Peter Drucker, Dr. Elisabeth Kübler-Ross, Stephen Covey, and more, including my old friends, Dr. Craig Miller and John Stewart!

My mentor, Dr. William Glasser, taught me in my early therapeutic and psychology training that all behavior has three dimensions: thinking, feeling, and doing. When one aligns with those dimensions, they can enjoy the fullness of their life and relationships. In leadership, we must learn to *think* like a leader, *feel* like a leader, and *do* the things a leader must do. In doing so, we begin to learn that our life starts with desires of having, and once we begin to have, we focus on doing things with what we have. Finally, as we reach maturity, the light switches on, and we realize that the most important stage in life is *being*.

In other words, *who* you are is so much more important than what you *do*.

I also strongly believe that there is a difference between a *job* and a *calling*. Over the years, I opened my speeches by asking my audiences what comes to mind when they hear the words "job" and "calling." Generally, they respond that a job involves tasks that need to be done and some sense of obligation. As for calling, they all seem to include the idea that what they do is fueled by a deep passion. Those ideas gave rise to another famous "Lumpkinism" that reflects John Stewart: "There is a difference between a job and a calling . . . one you *do* and one you can't stop *doing*."

In John's book, you will read about a man who exemplifies passion and the difference between a person who performs a "job" and one who is "called." I was fascinated when my friend and fellow consultant Dr. Craig Miller introduced me to John and I was exposed to his calling. As you embark on John's journey with him, you will learn what passion does in the heart of a leader—how it expresses itself in results, in out-of-the-box thinking, and in learning that the most important four-letter word in the English language is not "love," as most people would think; rather, it is "risk." (You cannot even love unless you are willing to risk!)

John's is a personal and professional story about risk, love, leadership, life-changing decisions, service, ethics, integrity, courage, confidence, and commitment—all critical attributes of a real, *called* leader. You will meet the John I know and come to appreciate that who he is, is even more important and inspiring than what he did.

We all wrestle with four cosmic questions in our lives: Who am I? Where am I going? What am I doing here? And what difference do I make?

These questions visit us all at various times in our journey of life and strangely never stay answered. You will learn how many times and ways John has dealt with these cosmic questions so far. Hopefully, when traveling with him in this story, you will ask them for yourself as well.

We are all pilgrims on a journey, and on our journey, we will meet other pilgrims as well. In their stories, we will find guidance, courage, determination, inspiration, and clarity of purpose. I am personally grateful that my pilgrim path crossed John's, and his mine. I am also confident that when you put down this book, you too will be grateful for such a destined meeting.

G. Dan Lumpkin, CMC, PhD
President of Lumpkin & Associates

INTRODUCTION

"You're a mess," the gastroenterologist said, looking over my charts. "You're going to be dead within three months."

That's when he told me that I had stage 3 cirrhosis and needed a liver transplant. I just looked at him, completely baffled. Only a year prior, all of my labs came back near normal. Both my A1C levels and liver enzymes were in good condition—nothing about my health raised any red flags, yet here I was, lying on an ER bed, shocked and in pain.

I recalled the events of the night. It was Tax Day, April 15. It was not going to be a late night for me, however, since I filed all my taxes ages ago. So, I said good night to Bently, my five-year-old English Cocker Spaniel, and happily went to bed at 11 p.m., ready to get some sleep and wake up as late as I wanted—one of the many perks of a retired life. Little did I expect, I woke up in just a few hours with a searing pain in my abdomen. Thinking the hiatal hernia I had years earlier might've flared up again, I took some antacids and tried to go back to sleep.

But this was pain like I never experienced before. At 3 a.m., I realized something was seriously wrong. On a pain scale, I was a 10. I called 911 immediately. Soon, four ambulances and a fire truck pulled up to my doorstep. Mind you, I had just moved into my new home in Charleston, and while I had briefly waved to a few of my neighbors, I didn't know anyone well enough to wake them up in the middle of the night. Funnily enough, I later found out that my neighbor's father, who suffers from insomnia, *was* awake that late and watched as the EMT wheeled me into the ambulance.

I was in such terrible pain that I didn't even think to lock my door or grab my wallet. All that went through my mind was pain, pain, pain. The EMTs practically had to pull me off the ambulance ceiling to inject me with morphine and fentanyl. *Twice.* That's how much it escalated. Even after all that, it took 12 hours in the emergency room at the nearby hospital to control the pain. They hooked me up to IVs in both of my arms, with medication being titrated through them to give me some relief. Doctors and nurses moved about, but through the daze, I could only recognize blurs of scrubs and incoherent speech. Then, just when the pain was slowly beginning to recede and I *finally* began to doze off, one of the nurses shook me awake.

"Mr. Stewart, we need to take you for a CT scan."

I almost begged them to let me just sleep.

They performed a lot of blood work and then an echocardiogram to check if I was having an aortic aneurysm—I was having pain in nearly the same area where the aorta passes through, so there was a big possibility that it had dissected. Finally, they administered the CT scan. That's when they found out that it was not an aortic aneurysm or a hiatal hernia flare-up after all.

I had stage 3 cirrhosis.

My liver was functioning at about 10 percent.

I had three months to live.

As the crotchety GI physician diagnosed me with chronic liver disease, I was completely taken aback. In April, all of my labs indicated normal liver function, but now, all of a sudden, my liver was shutting down.

There are about five ways that people can get cirrhosis, the most common being excessive alcohol consumption and parasites. While the possibility of my cirrhosis being caused by alcohol was low (as I usually only have an occasional social drink), I did enjoy sushi, sashimi, and raw oysters, which made it much more likely that parasites were the cause. However, the fifth cause of cirrhosis is hemochromatosis—and I had a genetic risk for it.

I had to stay in the hospital for four days while they monitored my pain and condition. While I waited, I essentially went through the five stages of grief, my thoughts constantly marked by *hows* and *whys*. I realized that I was experiencing feelings and thoughts that were similar to what I am used to seeing most patients go through.

During my 46-year career in the healthcare industry, I saw patients of all kinds, and those who didn't have long to live tended to go through a similar thought cycle: they planned to die because they never knew how things would change from one day to the next. I was in the same boat. Those four days were a time of such heavy, intense emotions that I couldn't reflect on how my entire career in healthcare might be coming to an end right where it began—in a hospital emergency room.

However, during those days of waiting, one thing became clear: no matter which hospital I was in, it never took much time for the caregivers to ask me suspiciously, "So, what do you do?" I suppose the way I interact with doctors and advocate for myself gives me away. After all, working in healthcare, starting as an ER registration clerk and eventually serving as the president of one of the largest medical groups in the country, has equipped me with a noticeable and unique skill or two.

Forty-six years in this wonderfully complex industry gave me the opportunity to serve in administrative roles where I could combine two of my greatest passions—taking care of others and improving the quality of service. In fact, my commitment to these two visions is so strong that even while I was lying in bed hooked up to monitors and an IV, I simply couldn't pass up an opportunity to make a difference.

The day before I got discharged from HCA, I noticed that while the doctors effectively communicated with each other, their communication with the nurses had somehow completely fallen through. I mean, *I* knew details about my care plan that the nurses weren't even told. When a patient knows more than the nurses, that's a sure sign something is not working right. I knew what had to be done. I even called up my niece and told her, "Thank goodness you're not here because I may embarrass you. Your Uncle John is about to go into CEO mode."

I asked the director of nursing and my chief hospitalist to come to my room. While they stood by the foot of my bed, I told them that if I were the CEO of this hospital, I would call the two of them and other key members of the care team to the boardroom, and we would not leave until we developed an action plan on how to improve care delivery.

I made it clear to the director of nursing: "There's no way I would've tolerated this standard of care in one of my hospitals. Neither should you." After they left the room, I looked around and realized that one of my nurses had listened to my whole lecture from the corner of the room. Before she left, she mouthed a quick thank you. I smiled, hoping that my comment might spur action and better results.

Soon, it was time to be discharged, but before then, they had to perform a paracentesis to remove fluid from my abdomen. They wheeled me into the ultrasound room where a nurse practitioner would perform the procedure.

When the nurse looked at me, she immediately said, "Oh, *you're* the CEO from 706!"

We laughed, and I joked about how my reputation precedes me. But before I could feel too good about myself, she proceeded to extract about two liters of fluid from my abdomen! The human body can be quite humbling.

As soon as the hospital discharged me, I scheduled an appointment with the primary care clinic at the Medical University of South Carolina, or MUSC. I needed a transplant . . . and fast. I reflected on the irony of this—not only had I seen transplants during my career, but I had also started transplant programs in hospitals. I had been fortunate enough to lead administrative teams in various healthcare systems, establish one of the nation's top cardiac care hospitals, support the acquisition of one of the country's largest medical groups, and instill a transformational culture of hospitality and patient care throughout every role in which I served.

Now, I was on the receiving end of the equation.

Chapter ONE

A Caregiver by Heart

Beaver Dam is a tiny town in Ohio County, Kentucky, that barely has a population of 2,500. To me, it's a truly special place. I grew up on a farm with a big garden and a big family. I remember my mother canning the green beans, corn, and tomatoes we harvested, an activity I always tried to weasel my way out of. What kid wants to can vegetables on a hot summer's day? But despite my best efforts, I found myself helping out, and so did all my neighbors, friends, and family. Thankfully, the cool watermelon, homemade ice cream, and big picnic meals always made it more bearable.

Giving was a recurrent theme in my family. My parents always took care of others: My father, a minister, fully dedicated himself to the service of our community. My mother provided for my family and everyone else, tirelessly working for our sake. My siblings and I gave our extra clothes and toys to kids less fortunate than us whenever we could. Beaver Dam had something to do with that too. The culture of service is ingrained in anyone who grew up in Western Kentucky—the unique mix of Southern and Midwestern charm, culture, and hospitality are the very essence of who we are.

One of six children, I was fortunate to have a family that was hardworking, loving, and most of all, musically genius. My father, Noble Stewart, grew up in a town next to Beaver Dam called Rosine, widely known as the birthplace of bluegrass music. It is here that he was raised, right next to Bill Monroe—the father of bluegrass music—and Charlie Monroe. My dad played in their band, The Kentucky Partners, and later went on tours with Charlie around the country, blessing people with their incredible, incredible music.

In fact, my dad would often tell me stories of his music-filled boyhood days. Once, he told me how he couldn't afford strings for his mandolin, so he took metal strands out of the screen porch and used them instead.

"We played until we bled," he said to me, and I looked up at him in awe. As a kid, I couldn't begin to comprehend that level of passion and dedication.

After the Monroe Brothers separated in 1938, Dad continued to play in Charlie's band, Charlie Monroe & the Kentucky Pardners. He wrote over 400 songs during his musical career and toured everywhere with the band in the 40s. One such tour brought him to Raleigh, North Carolina. Here, my dad felt a calling to the ministry. He had been thinking about it for a while, but this time, the calling was undeniable. He *had* to do it. When he told Charlie that the time had come for him to leave the band, Charlie joked, "So, you're going back to Kentucky to drink sassafras tea?"

In an effort to make him stay, Charlie brought out a suitcase full of fan mail, all addressed to "Noble Stewart."

My dad looked at him, surprised. He never knew. Charlie had hidden those letters for years.

While my dad always thrived in the glow of his audiences' praise and admiration, his calling to the ministry was simply too strong to ignore. Though he regretted leaving his music career, he found his place in the church and embraced the positive affirmations he received from his congregation. The musician in him never went away, of course. He simply passed it down to his six children.

All six of us Stewart kids were not only adept at singing but also at playing multiple instruments. I loved playing the piano, the acoustic guitar, and the bass guitar. But the best part was that music meant family time; we taught each other, and we played and sang together. It was my father, older sister, and older brother who taught me how to play instruments. Music was what bound us together, with my dad always acting as the conductor. In our household, a musical career was the norm. I started to play bass guitar and sing for a Southern gospel group called the Regals with my sister and her husband when I was barely a teenager. We toured around in a modified Greyhound bus and performed in churches and auditoriums. To this day, my love and appreciation for Southern gospel runs deep. It was my whole life at the time, after all.

Naturally, with music being such a constant presence in my childhood, I treasured the radio. Some days, I sat firmly planted in my father's car, listening to WLS on AM radio, trying to "escape." Later, when it was time for college, I chose to pursue a degree in mass communications at Western Kentucky University, with the intention of going into radio and TV broadcasting.

While interstate highways now make it easier to commute from Bowling Green to Louisville, Kentucky, it was nothing short of exhausting during those days. I had to drive an hour and a half or so to Louisville, perform with the Regals, and then commute back and attend classes. By that point, the Regals had grown so much and performed so often that commuting no longer made sense. I decided to just move to Louisville and stay with my sister and her husband for a while until I got settled.

While the weekends were spent performing, I needed something to do on the weekdays, now that I wasn't attending WKU. I wasn't too picky about it either—I just needed a job, something that could help me be more independent. My sister, who worked at Norton Children's Hospital in radiology, took me in one day and led me straight to the HR office. The head of human resources at the time was Mr. Terrell. He looked at me, a young man barely old enough to sign a form without needing permission from his parents, and said there was an entry-level position available as a registration clerk in the ER.

"Do you want it?" he asked.

I had no idea what that meant, but I knew it was a job. And a job was all I needed.

"That sounds great," I said. "When do I start?"

He called the supervisor and took me down to meet the manager of the emergency room registration area. She interviewed me and hired me on the spot.

I started a few days later, and *boy*, was it a job. This was way before computers, of course, so I was dealing with stacks and stacks of forms on the daily—papers that needed to be handed over, written in, checked, signed, and filed. I filled out so many forms that I can even tell you the codes, 46 years later. The code for the Kentucky Blue Cross Blue Shield was 011310107. You can take that to the bank.

I also remember my hourly pay: $2.98. With that wage, I saved up enough money to buy my first car, got approved for a loan, and moved to a beautiful studio apartment downtown! That's right. Try buying a latte with that amount today.

While I worked at the hospital on the weeknights (I was on the evening shift), I still performed with the Regals on the weekends. I never compromised on either one—I gave both my all. I started to develop some key personal values that have shaped me into the person I am today: always aiming for high standards, working hard, being on time, and staying consistent. It didn't take long for my work ethic to catch the attention of the vice president of ambulatory services, Mr. John Pratt, as well as my manager and my supervisor.

One day, Mr. Pratt called me into his office and presented an incredible opportunity: they wanted to start a first-of-its-kind urgent care. (Until this point, the hospital took on the role of an emergency trauma center as opposed to a clinic.) They wanted to put *me* in charge of setting that up. I couldn't help but be proud; it was the first of many times I would receive a work-based promotion, but the recognition for a job well done never loses its significance. I was also thrilled to be given a leadership role. I've always had the ability to develop friendships easily, especially relationships based on mutual trust and respect, so an opportunity to get involved with a team and work with them to establish an urgent care unit just sounded incredible.

At the time, I was living fairly close to the University of Louisville School of Medicine, and during my evening shift, I got to meet with a lot of health practitioners whom I often joined for drinks at the end of the day. This hyper-medical area must've rubbed off on me because, when a couple of respiratory therapists I spent time with started recommending I go to respiratory therapy school, I seriously considered it. Norton Children's had a wonderful tuition reimbursement program I could take advantage of, and all they wanted in return was a commitment to work there once I was done.

Well, I thought, *I'm gonna need a job anyway, so why not?*

Long story short, I went to respiratory therapy school. Since Kentucky did not have the Respiratory Therapy Licensure Act enforced yet, I could work in the respiratory therapy department after my first year of training. So, I transferred over from the emergency room to work in med-surg. I was able to work directly with patients for the first time and was soon administering breathing, nebulizer, and oxygen therapy treatments. Since I was often the respiratory therapist assigned to the fourth floor, I was given a beeper to carry in case there was a trauma in the emergency room. Not to be crude, but whenever there was an emergency that needed me to go down, it was *great* because I got to work with the people I was closest to once again. It's the small things, especially in an environment as stressful as an emergency room. The presence of teammates you trust can make a huge difference. Once again, my hard work and commitment paid off: I was promoted to the position of assistant shift supervisor—and I wasn't even old enough to drink yet!

CAMARADERIE IN THE EMERGENCY ROOM

As my respiratory therapist career progressed, it became harder and harder to balance it with my music career. Deciding between two passions, two diverging forks in the road, is never easy.

The Regals were starting to garner national attention, and our tours increased exponentially. I'd often board our custom Greyhound bus on a Saturday, ride to a different city and perform, travel all the way back at night, and then arrive in Louisville early the following morning, just in time for my seven o'clock clinical rotation. Sometimes, I even asked the bus driver to just drop me off straight at the hospital!

Even though I did not want to pick between the two, the time had come. I could no longer avoid making the decision. The positive affirmations and validations I received from the doctors, neonatologists, therapists, and nurses were enough to help me realize that I was making a real difference in the hospital. It was the hardest thing in the world to tell my family I was going into healthcare—everyone else had pursued music, so I was the odd one out. I knew I was making the right decision, however. The chance to serve patients while supporting my teammates on their shifts was incredibly rewarding. I felt like I was tapping into my caregiver nature more and more every day.

Of course, I could never forget the patients I worked with, some of whom come to mind when I remember the particularly harsh tornadoes that hit Louisville one year. Since we were the only pediatric trauma center in the whole area, a mass amount of injured adults and children alike flooded our facilities.

One child, whom I still think about from time to time even today, had a stick about a foot long impaled straight through his arm—that was how powerful the tornado had been. Another time, a child who was hit by a train came into the trauma center, and the injury was so extreme that I barely held out hope. His face, from his nose all the way down to his lower jaw, was completely pulled back. He was only eight. Remarkably, the child was alert. *And thank god, he was breathing.* As the respiratory therapist on call, I would've been completely helpless if he wasn't because there was no way to resuscitate him—the injury had completely blocked any access to his airway. The boy pulled through and survived, although he did need multiple reconstructive surgeries over the years to fix his oropharynx and mouth regions.

Treating patients who had been through such serious trauma naturally developed a tie between us. No one but healthcare professionals can appreciate the bond one develops with a patient. It's a truly remarkable and unforgettable feeling.

After I completed my second year of training, I was permitted to work in the intensive care unit. To this day, the layout and design of the ground floor—which consisted of the ICUs, operating rooms, and radiology and clinical labs—enabled the most efficient floor system that I've ever worked in. Even though the building opened in 1974, no modern hospital I've seen can even come close to achieving the efficiency of Norton Children's ground floor. This was even more significant when you realize that at the time, CT scans weren't even invented! To take an X-ray, we had to wheel in a huge X-ray machine with gigantic plates that were bulky, heavy, and incredibly inconvenient to move around. I'm glad I recognized the efficiency of the layout then because, years later, when I was in charge of designing and building the St. Vincent Heart Center in Indiana, I applied some of these architectural and organizational elements to strengthen efficiency, flow, and order. Of course, back then, I had no idea that I would one day utilize my observations and mental notes in such a monumental way. I simply admired the ingenuity of the designer and felt lucky to work in such an intentionally organized space.

Once I started working as a full-time respiratory therapist, I would do month-long rotations in different departments. One month, I would work in the pediatric ICU, the next one in med-surg, and the one after that in the adult ICU. After a while, my shift supervisor finally decided that it was time for me to move to the department that demanded the highest proficiency and rigorous training: the newborn intensive care unit.

Now, here's the thing about newborn ICUs: everyone hated working there because it was so incredibly intense and, at times, heartbreaking. Every single therapist dreaded their newborn ICU rotation. That is, every therapist but me—I hated the third floor, which housed the burn unit and pediatric oncology. If there was one thing I could not stand, it was watching children suffer. So, once I got used to the newborn ICU, I happily traded rotations with all the other therapists so that I never had to go up to the third floor again. I spent most of my time in the newborn ICU, and everyone was happy to let me. The neonatologist and the nurses grew accustomed to having me around. Each day, I got better at understanding the system, working with the team, and earning their trust. Soon, I was one of the first therapists to exclusively specialize in newborn ICU and one of the only four therapists trained in administering ECMO, or extracorporeal membrane oxygenation.

Before I knew it, I was assigned to a new, impactful team of respiratory therapists who specialized in newborn ICU, tasked with starting and developing the neonatal transport initiative. We created a process that allowed us to fly throughout the state of Kentucky, Southern Indiana, and certain parts of West Virginia to pick up infants and bring them back to Norton Children's Hospital.

This was a much-needed service since we had the only level-four newborn ICU in the entire state of Kentucky and the expertise and equipment to treat extremely serious and acute cases. In fact, years later, my niece had a baby in Bowling Green, Kentucky, who started having unforeseen complications. The neonatal transport team that I helped start was then able to swoop in, pick up the baby, and provide life-saving treatment. It was an incredibly stressful time for us all, but when I told her over the phone, "Don't worry, your Uncle John started this program," it seemed to make her more comfortable. I never imagined that there would be a day when something I did at the age of 21 would allow me to see my great-niece grow into a beautiful, healthy child and start elementary school.

The neonatal transport team was a service that helped many families and infants, not just my own, and made infant emergency healthcare more accessible, even during times when it seemed hopeless.

The camaraderie in an emergency room is unparalleled. No one but the people who have been with you as you treated and supported patients through the most stressful situations can trust you to the extent of life and death. One situation in particular revealed to me the extent of complete trust and faith my team had in me—something I never have, and never will, take for granted.

At the time, it was one of the most touching moments of my entire life.

FIGHTING THE STORM

It was my very last neonatal transport in Louisville, Kentucky. A major snowstorm had hit us, and when we received a call for twin infants to be picked up as soon as possible, the FAA (Federal Aviation Administration) told us there was no way we could fly there due to the unsafe weather conditions. The winds were blowing with a fury I'd never seen, and the snowstorm was only just picking up speed. The people on the other end of the phone call, the twins' family, were crying. Without our help, there was nothing that could be done. The twins would die.

We had no idea what to do. It was a terrible situation, completely out of our control. Then, one of the doctors who was on call, Dr. Shot, stood up. He had served as an army doctor, and he knew very well the boundaries of life and death, hope and hopelessness. He wasn't going to give in without a fight.

"If I was still in the army," he said, standing up tall, "I would be asking for volunteers."

The seriousness of the situation, the very real possibility of death while making the trip, meant it was no longer only limited to respiratory therapists—they needed any help they could get. He was met with silence. It was a huge ask and an impossible decision.

One of the nurses said, her voice strong and determined, "I will go if John Stewart goes."

I stared, trying to process what she had just said. I could hardly refuse. The trust she placed in me was something I simply could not let down. At that moment, I knew what I had to do.

The snow and storm blew us sideways, and the plane swayed dangerously as we flew to Paducah. It was turbulence and chaos like you couldn't imagine. I couldn't believe we had made it when we landed on a runway. There was an ambulance waiting for us, and it quickly took us to the hospital. We waited for a few hours, letting the worst of the storm pass us, and then took the flight back, consisting of a nurse, a doctor, a respiratory therapist, and two infant twins who needed immediate care. On the way back to Norton Children's, one of the infants' breathing tubes became dislodged. I had to re-intubate—a delicate process not meant to be done in a swaying plane, with the winds and the storm threatening to throw us all off. It was a pressure I had never faced before. A vulnerable life rested in my hands. Somehow, I reintubated successfully. They had a fighting chance.

After we finally reached the hospital, the two infants had to be kept in the newborn ICU for over a year. But they made it. They were able to go back home. We had saved two infant lives. Even today, I marvel at how we managed it. I could never take credit for it. A higher power, something bigger than me and bigger than all of us, must've guided us through that storm and helped us save the twins. There is simply no other explanation. For years later, I received Christmas cards from the infants' parents; their mother was, ironically, a respiratory therapist herself.

The emotions that the trip brought out in me cannot be put into words. The positive affirmation, the highs of seeing my patients thrive and overcome impossible complications, and the mutual trust and respect that was such a big part of the neonatal transport team and the hospital as a whole—it all validated that if we relied on each other, we could pull through and save lives time and time again. I will always be grateful that my career brought me to the point where I could experience and contribute to such important work every single day.

Chapter TWO

A Life of Continuous Learning

Life was going well in Louisville. But I had only moved there because of my career with the Regals. Now that I had quit singing with the band, staying in Louisville started to make less sense. Besides, I was approaching a transition point. My love for traveling and exploring new places only just started to raise its head again when a few of my friends in San Francisco reached out to me and asked me to visit. That seemed as fun a prospect as any, so during the holidays, I took a week's vacation and flew out to California.

On a whim, I decided to check out the newborn ICU at the Children's Hospital in San Francisco. On that tour, I had the pleasure of meeting Dr. Joyce Peabody. When I talk about life opening doors to opportunities you never see coming, it is this day that always comes to mind. Dr. Peabody and I got to talking about my career so far and my experiences at Norton Children's, particularly my contribution to starting the neonatal transport team. When I was chatting with the other doctors and nurses, she stepped out into the hall with the director of respiratory therapy. A few minutes later, they came back in and offered me a job on the spot as a respiratory therapist at their newborn ICU.

To tell you I felt deeply flattered would be an understatement. I didn't bother hesitating because the answer was clear. I said yes. A few weeks later, I was confidentially told I would take over as assistant director of respiratory therapy. As assistant director, I would be in charge of the newborn ICU and the pediatric ICU, a clear step up from my position at Louisville. This incredible opportunity also happened to come at a time when I was searching for an escape—from my family, from trauma, and in many ways, from the reality of a horrible tragedy.

Months before, my older sister had been killed in a car accident. My family and I just didn't know how to deal with her death. And I coped with it terribly.

So, I ran.

A new city felt like a welcome change, one that I believed would help me grieve the loss.

A CULTURE OF QUALITY

I initially started at the San Francisco Children's Hospital as a respiratory therapist. This allowed me to familiarize myself with the team and their procedures while the administration worked out its structure. As a respiratory therapist working the night shift, I soon "earned my scrubs," so to speak. The other nurses, therapists, and physicians were able to assess my caliber and knack for newborn ICU, and before long, a relationship of mutual respect and trust developed. Once again, I was blessed with great teammates and an even better work environment. A few months later, when an assistant director position opened up, I smoothly transitioned into that role, knowing I had the full support of my colleagues.

The culture here really stood out to me. In Louisville, the neonatologists were all men, whereas, in San Francisco, they were all women. The ones in charge were Dr. Peabody; Dr. June Brady, an older, gray-haired lady with reading glasses and a British accent whose appearance always conjured up the image of a librarian in my mind; and Dr. Toshi Hirada, an Asian-American woman who exuded an air of strict rigidity and extreme focus on even the smallest of details. People would literally stand up straighter when she entered a room.

Together, their intense attention to quality and safety elevated the organization to a realm of superior care. Here, I felt like my vision for quality healthcare perfectly aligned with the protocols they had in place.

I also dabbled more intensively in research than I ever previously had the opportunity to. I was, after all, in the presence of great minds: Dr. Brady had developed the first totally monitored beds for infants, hooked up to every piece of monitoring equipment necessary, such as chromatographs and EEG machines. Then, there was Dr. Peabody who was engaged in research in Germany with Dräger, and their team was credited for inventing and doing the initial research on transcutaneous monitoring. To have the incredible opportunity to do research with these brilliant professionals was, as you can imagine, intimidating, thrilling, and deeply gratifying all at once.

As assistant director of respiratory care for the newborn ICU, I dealt with staffing, human resources, continuing education, and equipment, all while acting as a content expert and resource for not only respiratory therapists but also neonatologists and anyone else who needed a second opinion. Since I had the expertise of helping develop the neonatal transport team while at Louisville, my superiors in San Francisco charged me with establishing a pediatric transport team. (They had a neonatal transport team for newborns already up and running even before I joined.)

My responsibilities expanded almost overnight. I had a lot more people depending on me and my expertise, and my administrative commitments gained an elevated importance.

As I stepped into my new role, I was on somewhat of a learning curve myself. It was during this time that Medicare came out with diagnostic-related groupings (DRGs), which meant our entire payment system had to change. Earlier, respiratory therapy was nothing less than a cash cow—we billed for the procedures we conducted, and there was no standardized, one-for-all fee to speak of. However, with the implementation of DRGs, we had to set the same fee regardless of which treatment we provided to the patient.

During the advanced period before this could go into effect, I was in charge of gathering information and quantifying the financial impact of this for our department. I went in and reviewed every single chart associated with a Medicare patient and categorized them according to the DRG group they would fall into. Obviously, this wasn't the most digitally advanced time—all I had by my side was the Commodore 64, the very first computer I ever worked on, infinitely famous for its affordability and sheer bulkiness. My team and I developed our own supply management program on this computer, and this was the main reason I later went to Seton Medical Center as a consultant: to implement it in their respiratory therapy department.

I'm a huge advocate for embracing learning curves, no matter how steep they are. Often, by going down this path of learning and discovery, you'll find new strengths and talents. I never imagined I would be so interested or passionate about developing supply management programs or working digitally—but there I was, incredibly enthused by it all! It was an excellent opportunity to develop new skills and also open up potential future opportunities for myself, even though I had none of these expectations going in.

Quickly, I settled into the fast-paced world at Children's Hospital. I picked up their dedication to providing quality care and familiarized myself with their various protocols. A protocol that differed from Louisville was the unit's unique approach called *minimal handling*. Say we had a critically ill infant, a vulnerable and tiny thing weighing no more than 480 grams. Such infants' conditions can change immediately with no warning signs. The only influence that could potentially save them, in these cases, is a physician, nurse, or respiratory therapist who works closely with that specific infant, is well aware of the infant's unique idiosyncrasies, and can spot when things are about to turn for the worse. It is unreasonable to expect every nurse, doctor, and therapist to be comprehensively well-versed with each one of the 25 infants that occupy the NICU. So, having a designated team that works with an infant ensures continuity of care.

I was on one such team for an infant who had severe pulmonary hypertension and meconium aspiration. A beautiful, beautiful baby who had perfect weight and function in every other regard. Sadly, due to the meconium aspiration, she experienced a complete loss of brain function and stayed that way for months after, only her heart beating away and keeping her alive. Just like the family from Paducah, Kentucky, I became familiar with this family as well, the mother being a prominent politician. They were incredibly attentive parents, and it was heartbreaking to let them know that their baby passed. It's always difficult to be on cases like these, especially when you develop such intimate connections with the infants and their parents, being on a dedicated team that works with them and them only. However, the minimal handling protocol also allows for trust to develop between the parents and the team, which is indispensable.

For every negative patient care experience that I went through, thank goodness I had hundreds that turned out well. If these weren't the numbers, I probably would've quit my job a long, long time ago. I was not able to emotionally handle working in departments like pediatric oncology where you need to walk into the unit knowing that most of the kids will not make it. It's witnessing traumatic patient care situations like these that made us realize the importance of behavioral health and pastoral care for the entire team—it was crucial to provide them with resources to process and decompress after particularly hard cases. Thankfully, these days, treatment and medical care have come a long way since the 70s.

I extended this emotional understanding and moral support to other departments as well, especially whenever times got tough. And what a tough time it was: AIDS had just been diagnosed and reported for the first time—in fact, in those early days, we didn't even have a name for it. In 1982, *The New York Times* published an article that labeled the new immune system disorder "gay-related immune deficiency" (GRID), considering the disease primarily affected homosexual men.[1] This branding of AIDS then led the public to refer to it as "the gay plague" for many years after, despite the multiple ways the disease can be transmitted and to whom it can be transmitted.

Our hospital had a few of the first AIDS patients in the entire country. Research was in full swing, but at the time, no one had a clue what was going on. As assistant director, I found myself on the frontlines when the first AIDS patients came in. And because we didn't know what it was or how it was transmitted, instead of assigning staff to care for them, those of us in supervisory positions volunteered. We took all the precautions we could: I'm talking a full gown-up of face shields and gloves and booties. We wore more protective gear than even those in the operating room. And while many people in healthcare hesitated to approach the bedsides of those with AIDS, I knew providing such care was my calling, and I felt guided by a higher power.

San Francisco was a dark place to live and work during this time. The only other period in history that I can liken it to would be ancient Europe during the Black Death—except this disease affected a grossly underrepresented group of people who were continually denied necessary care due, in large part, to prejudice and misunderstanding. We lost two of our hospital administrators and several doctors at the Children's Hospital. As for my friends and acquaintances, I stopped counting after 50 deaths. The impact AIDS had on San Francisco was devastating to an unfathomable number of people; from there, it only expanded and moved throughout the country.

This is why I have so much respect for Dr. Anthony Fauci, who started to make incredible breakthroughs in our understanding of HIV/AIDS and treatment options from the very first day of its outbreak. As he says in an *Advocate* interview, he and his team may have been "putting Band-Aids on hemorrhages," but it's this difficult work that contributed to the progress against HIV around the world—and why, as he says, it may be possible to end the outbreak by 2030 if we continue "shaking the cage" and promoting funding for anti-AIDS programs.[2] I can only look at the work of Dr. Fauci, both past and present, and consider him a saint.

VINCENTIAN VALUES

I had another learning experience at San Francisco Children's Hospital—probably one of the biggest, scariest moments of my life. One time, I was performing chest physiotherapy on an infant, zoned in on the task at hand. I had my arms through the two holes in the incubator while a nurse was on the other side, getting some other medications ready for the baby. After performing the necessary procedures, a small amount of saline needs to be injected into their endotracheal tube to loosen the secretions before they can be suctioned out. I prepared my syringe full of saline, put it on top of the baby's incubator, and turned around to silence the alarm on the transcutaneous monitor. I barely glanced at the top of the incubator before picking up a syringe and injecting its contents down the infant's endotracheal tube. It took all of two seconds for me to realize something was wrong. I turned around, looked at the incubator, and looked at the nurse who was working right across from me. Her face was in shock, and I suppose, so was mine. I was horror-struck. I quickly found out that the nurse had drawn up a syringe full of sedatives for the baby but had left it on the incubator, unlabeled. And my syringe was next to hers, also unlabeled. In my hurry, I had picked up the wrong syringe. *I had just injected a sedative into the infant's ET tube*. I felt shaken to the very core of my being.

Only one thought seemed to flash in my mind, again and again: *I killed that baby*.

We immediately got in touch with the clinical pharmacist to look into some research and figure out what to do. Of course, by then, I already tried to suction out as much of the sedative as I could, injected some saline, and then suctioned it out again, trying to clear the sedative from the baby's lungs. Thankfully, we found out that the sedative will not cross over the membranes in the lung. I breathed a sigh of relief, but I was still in a state of shock over what I had just done. I could not *believe* I let that happen. I had almost jeopardized a young life, all because I looked away for a moment and didn't label my syringe. From that moment on, I felt fixated very strongly on quality and safety, a lesson I applied throughout the rest of my career. I didn't ever want to create even a possibility of something like that happening again, to myself or to anyone else.

My re-energized quest for quality spurred me to confront a few flaws of San Francisco Children's Hospital that I had been trying to look past, the biggest issue being the unethical behavior of leadership at the time. I was getting increasingly uncomfortable and frustrated, so I begrudgingly decided to look for another opportunity.

Thankfully, I was well acquainted with the leaders of a Daughters of Charity organization: Mary's Help Hospital. I had already been approached by them to help implement the supply management program we had developed, so I transitioned into working at Mary's Help Hospital (now renamed Seton Medical Center) as a consultant.

It was here, at this Daughters of Charity organization, that I was asked to be a part of the development of "Vincentian values." I had an opportunity to truly transform an organization's quality and hospitality values, something that I became progressively more passionate about. We took the teachings of the patron saints of the Daughters of Charity, St. Vincent de Paul and St. Louise de Marillac, and developed them into the foundational values of the organization.

From being helpless in effecting ethical change in my later months at San Francisco Children's Hospital to developing an ethical framework centered on quality and patient care at Seton, I finally had the opportunity to tap into what was near and dear to my heart.

As I began training the physicians, nurses, and staff in these Vincentian values, I discovered another pleasure of mine: teaching and providing space for continuous education. I enjoyed working with various departments, offering advice, and problem-solving where I could. Whenever people said something to the effect of, "This is going to bring our system crashing down," I would respond with, "Daughters of Charity have been around for 400 years. They've survived this 'small' thing called the plague. I'm sure we can get through this."

Once I set up that perspective, finding solutions didn't seem all that difficult.

Sadly, my time at Mary's Help Hospital ("Our Lady of 280," as we lovingly called her due to the hospital's location right next to I-280) was close to an end. One of the vice presidents I worked with told me about an opening at O'Connor Hospital in San Jose, and I applied. It was another Daughters of Charity organization, and by then, I realized that Daughters of Charity was where I belonged. When I got the job, I was thrilled.

I relocated to San Jose where I met Kathy Rowan, the then-vice president of O'Connor, who soon became one of my mentors. While I had accepted the offer, I only realized when

I started that there were not one but *three* open positions: director of cardiology, director of respiratory therapy, and a combination of the first two into the brand new position of cardiac service line administrator. You must know me by now; *of course*, I picked the new, higher-stakes position and became the very first person to serve as a cardiac service line administrator at O'Connor Hospital.

I had to agree when Kathy told me that I would fit this position best: the responsibilities included overseeing multiple departments, coordinating with everyone from nurses to neurologists to physicians and cardiologists, and handling organizational and administrative roles as well. It was a loaded job, but the fact that I had always been able to develop relationships with different members of the organization gave me ease. Sure enough, within no time, I developed relationships of mutual trust and respect with everyone, including the neurologists at the time, who were hard to win over.

In this organization, I once again got the opportunity to develop new systems and nurture existing ones. We tripled our open-heart surgery volume and even started our very first sleep center. (Although, we were a long way from overtaking our nearest competitor, Stanford University, the mecca of sleep centers, anytime soon.) We went from about 200 open-heart surgeries in a year to over 600, giving us the title for most surgeries. Even Stanford University performed only about 300 per year because of the Bay Area's high number of open-heart surgery programs.

Today, I cannot believe the extraordinary opportunity I had to hone my skills and engage in continuous learning as I tried to manage multiple departments—cardiology, pulmonary, respiratory therapy, and neurodiagnostic—all the while working to improve protocols and develop new ones. Leading, I was starting to realize, was another passion of mine.

Sadly, toward the end of my five-and-a-half years at O'Connor, my mother fell ill. She lived with one of my brothers at the time, but her condition was steadily worsening. I wanted to move closer to her, just in case.

I was soon approached by a recruiter who represented a reputable hospital in Atlanta and asked to interview me for the position of vice president of cardiology. I flew out and visited the hospital, but no sooner had I stepped in than I realized it just wouldn't be a good fit for me.

Looking back, I'm glad I turned down that offer. Not long after declining the position, I received another opportunity from a different Daughters of Charity hospital in Pensacola. Accepting their offer, quite literally, transformed my entire career, allowing me to take on responsibilities, risks, and challenges like never before. I had no way of knowing this then, but my time there became the beating heart of my professional journey.

Chapter THREE
Mission, Vision, Values

Walking into Jay Hardman's office for the first time, I immediately noticed how the space reminded me so much of those old-fashioned corporate offices you see in movies. Heck, it even had a fully stocked bar, repurposed out of a cabinet, that sat against the wall. Never before in my career had I seen such an office, especially not in a hospital!

Just by entering the room, I could tell that Jay's office was a direct reflection of the control and dominance he exerted over all the hospital's operations. While he was the COO of Sacred Heart Health System, he performed all the duties of a CEO and essentially ran the whole ship. Even though I had already been interviewed by Ron Bailey (my direct supervisor at the time), human resources, and Patrick Schlenker (who, like Jay, was an ex-military officer and ran the hospital with him like an army institution), I was not guaranteed the position until Jay gave his stamp of approval. It was for this interview that I was in his office. Thankfully, he saw the abilities and experience in me that everyone else had appreciated so far. I got the go-ahead and officially started at Sacred Heart as the service line administrator.

The position gave me the opportunity to gain the trust and respect of senior leadership. It solidified my self-belief and validated my passion for leadership, affirmations that motivated me to give my all to the organization and take charge.

One particular meeting comes to mind. As the service line administrator, I quickly developed great relationships with the cardiologists, surgeons, and pulmonologists. This had not gone unnoticed. At the meeting, we discussed if we needed to pull in a consulting firm to serve as an intermediary between our doctors and the hospitals and deal with our changing contracts.

When the topic came up, Jay Hardman immediately looked in my direction, pointed a finger at me, and said, "John, you have the best relationship with the physicians. I want you to have full responsibility and the latitude to make this work."

Then, he turned to look at others and said, "And I want you guys to stay out of John's way."

With that pronouncement, he cleared all doubt of who was to lead the charge of building the Heart and Vascular Institute. Having that level of impact was incredibly rewarding and a fine opportunity to put my years of experience into action. I didn't miss a beat. It took us nine months to fully form the institute. We immediately developed a gainsharing program and hired a consulting firm, Health Evolutions (where I would eventually join as a consultant myself). I met with Jay weekly to update him on my team's progress, and it was incredible how much Jay, my team, and I were able to accomplish by working together in perfect sync.

We grew exponentially, reminding me of my time at O'Connor. When I joined, Sacred Heart performed 350 open-heart surgeries per year; with the institute, our numbers increased to 1,100. We *tripled* our volume, a success I owe to our infrastructure, collective culture, and shared vision.

Every day, I aimed to serve others as part motivational speaker, part pillar of support, and part visionary. It was primarily this skill set that fueled my efforts as the Daughters of Charity organization steadily moved toward merging with the Sisters of St. Joseph Health System, set to create the Ascension National Health System in 1999 and become its own public juridic person.

Before this merge and another acquisition with the Carondelet Health Network could occur, Daughters of Charity and Sacred Heart wanted to initiate a pilot program that would develop training processes to ensure consistent and shared mission, vision, and values for the soon-to-be Ascension Health. After all, with multiple religious orders coming together, there were bound to be a few fundamental differences. To make the future of the organization work, it was necessary for all the physicians, administrators, and staff to see eye-to-eye when it came to the core set of organizational beliefs.

One overarching mission and value system had to be developed well before any acquisitions could take place.

SERVE THOSE WHO SERVE OTHERS

By this point, I had embraced my passion for creating foundational elements of successful organizations, namely the mission, vision, and values. I was asked to help develop this pilot program and be one of the initial trainers, along with Pippa Nicholson, a nurse by background who ran the women's service line. While a dedicated team assembled the programs, Pippa and I led the servant leadership training together as a dyad.

One of the lessons we taught was such a focal point of my philosophy that I can still remember the PowerPoint presentation slides, word for word: "A servant leader is one who serves those who serve others," an idea expressed by Robert Greenleaf.[3] Servant leadership has become the essence of my leadership style; it is who I am, how I lead, and the way I teach others. Later, I even went as far as becoming certified as a coach and mentor through the John Maxwell training program where servant leadership is one of the most significant principles.

While this pilot training program became a huge piece of my personal and professional growth, I also had the opportunity to contribute to another equally impactful and fulfilling program: the formation of the chest pain center.

Dr. William Doty led an effort through the Florida chapter of the American College of Cardiology around palliative care at Sacred Heart and acted as the main driving force behind this initiative. While at Sacred Heart, Dr. Doty noticed that in the emergency room, patients would sometimes experience sudden heart attacks, but no one would notice them in time to provide appropriate care. Sacred Heart was an adult and pediatric trauma center, and as such, traumas were our specialty. However, heart attacks and other medical conditions, which could be just as acute as trauma, often did not receive necessary attention on account of the doctors and staff not responding to them with the same level of urgency as they did with trauma alerts. We knew we needed to develop a program to counter this, so Dr. Doty and I put our heads together to formulate a plan.

Dr. Doty conceptualized the idea to designate a few beds in the emergency room specifically for those experiencing chest pain or at risk for heart attacks—we were already doing something similar with the trauma beds, after all. We also became aware of someone else who had taken measures to solve this issue: Dr. Raymond Bahr at St. Agnes Hospital in Baltimore had developed the very first chest pain center at the time. To gain a better understanding, not only of the chest pain center's operating procedures but also of the need for them, we decided to send our medical director and a few of the emergency room staff to visit Dr. Bahr.

When they came back, the physicians, nurses, and the medical director were all beyond excited.

The medical director said, "John, now we get what you and Dr. Doty have been talking about. We need to develop and mirror the chest pain center concept. Only then can we treat heart attacks more efficiently." With that validation of our own thoughts, Dr. Doty and I began to establish the very first chest pain center in Florida. But a mountain already lay in our path: there was simply no space for it. Looking at the passion and energy of the team that had come back from observing the chest pain center in Baltimore though, Dr. Doty and I knew we couldn't give up. We needed to make this happen, one way or another. And our solution came in the form of a not-so-elegant storage room.

Was it below our expectations? Was it barely a space? Sure. But Dr. Doty and I remained motivated. If a storage room was all we could get, a storage room would be what we'd use to develop a service that our patients and staff desperately needed.

We quickly flew into motion, calling up architects and asking them to draw up plans for the storage room that would bring it up to code. Once all that was settled, we put in four (only four!) beds, and the Sacred Heart Chest Pain Center was open for business. Soon, the center and the hospital as a whole were doing so well that we got the approval and funding to develop an entire new wing!

EXPANDING EXPERTISE

Every project at Sacred Heart helped me hone my skills exponentially. The training pilot program allowed me to better learn how to bring people together, educate and mentor them, understand the motivations and values of each individual, and spot their strengths and collaborative abilities. The chest pain center development project deepened my problem-solving and leadership skills and demonstrated that continuous learning is always possible, especially if you're open to allowing your work to challenge you. Sometimes, a project can even open up a new avenue of passion that you were previously unaware of. It wasn't until I was a part of the information steering committee that I recognized my interest in all things technology implementation.

When Sister Irene Kraus, the CEO of Sacred Heart (and later one of my mentors and dear friends), asked me to represent our organization as one of the five ministries that made up the Daughters of Charity National Cardiac Database Steering Committee, I never imagined how deep a passion I'd have for technology and information systems. Or how this committee would introduce me to the incredible Brenda Erner, who would come into my life once again to partner with my team at the Heart Center of Indiana. As vice president of the Indiana Heart Institute (now called Navion), she and I would go on to have multiple discussions about data in healthcare and start initiatives in hospital systems to provide physicians with better access to accurate abstracted data. But that awaits us in the future.

At this time in Sacred Heart, I simply accepted my position on the national cardiac database as another responsibility and dedicated myself to doing the best work I could. We implemented an information system specific to respiratory therapy and cardiology, an undertaking that was anything but a one-and-done project.

Over the course of my time at Sacred Heart, we must've implemented and replaced the information systems binder about a dozen times, and each time, I was fortunate enough to find myself on the information steering committee. The role involved strategy, innovative problem-solving, and implementing technological solutions—all skills that I cultivated and polished during my 10 years there and continued to leverage throughout the rest of my career. In fact, in the present day, my interest in technology is one of the reasons why I sit on the board of Ascesis, an innovator of healthcare performance improvement software.

Just as important as it was for me to recognize and advance my own skills, I equally focused on supporting and encouraging the skills of others.

When I first started at Sacred Heart, I "inherited" Christine Blackmon as my assistant. As I settled in, the acting director of respiratory therapy approached me and shook her head disappointedly: "John, I think you're going to end up firing Christine because the quality of her work is just not up to standard."

I didn't let her analysis of Christine's ability cloud my judgments, and I'm glad I didn't. Soon after that interaction, I realized that not only was she a smart person, quick on the uptake, and great at implementing ideas, but she was also grossly underutilized by the organization. So, when I began working on the respiratory therapy information system, I asked Christine if she could take the lead in our efforts and support us in the CliniVision system's installment. She looked nervous.

Slowly, she asked, "Do you think I can?"

"I think you're somebody who needs a challenge," I said, optimistic. "If you're challenged, you will become an asset. And Sacred Heart could use an asset like you."

I must've convinced her because she jumped in with confidence and perseverance and blew the project out of the water. As a matter of fact, she was so good that everybody started relying on her and her expanding expertise, and they even started calling her Miss CliniVision!

Religious Inspiration

Sacred Heart is near and dear to my heart for one more reason: it was here that I officially converted to Catholicism. I was raised non-denominational, but being from Kentucky, my father typically performed in Baptist churches throughout my childhood. However, back when I quit the Regals and went into my education and healthcare full-time, I grew distant from the evangelical churches where we often performed and, by extension, from my faith as well.

I left the church then, but as I started to become more involved at Sacred Heart, where Catholicism influenced the core mission, vision, and values of the organization, I began to enjoy it—the homilies, the education, the prevailing harmony. Feeling a profound connection to the Catholic Church, I started the Rite of Christian Initiation of Adults (RCIA) program with Father Tom, the associate pastor at St. Peter and Paul Catholic Cathedral in Pensacola. As he would later admit to me, our RCIA class was one of the most difficult, considering three of us in attendance were all preachers' kids!

I vividly remember one day when, soon after I completed the RCIA program, I was sitting in the cafeteria at Sacred Heart. It was packed—there was a dedication service, and many of the CEOs and sisters were invited to attend. Enjoying my lunch with a few colleagues, I looked up from the table to see Sister Irene walking through the tables and heading straight toward me, like she was on a mission. I hadn't seen her in a while—she had been posted as the administrator for a provincial house in Emmitsburg and only traveled to Sacred Heart for the dedication service. Before I could compose myself, she was already at my table instructing me to stand up. Not sure what was happening, I did. And right there, in the middle of an overflowing cafeteria, she gave me a big hug.

"What was that for?" I said, surprised.

"I heard you completed the RCIA program," she said, smiling. I couldn't believe the news that I had finished the program and been baptized somehow reached her ears all the way in Emmitsburg! She was such an incredible mentor, friend, and religious inspiration. Even now, I can't help but think of her happiness for me fondly.

For a decade, I learned and developed leadership skills at Sacred Heart, and the opportunity to work with incredible people kept me motivated and eager to serve others. Eventually, however, a CEO change drastically altered the organization's culture. Before long, I realized that I was no longer a cultural fit in the space. My close relationships with physicians and nurses, a virtue that Sister Irene Kraus and Jay Hardman viewed as my biggest strengths, were seen as liabilities and threats to the new management.

In their words, I was "too close to the doctors."

I was taken aback. I was a service line administrator. What else did they expect? These relationships were a critical part of my job description! It was when management started pulling their power to implement self-serving changes in the organization that I finally realized where the hospital was headed: to a place where I could no longer effect positive change.

During this long tenure, I developed a great relationship with Steve Thomas, founder and president of Health Evolutions, as he had seen me take charge and strategize initiatives to great success. One day, he approached me.

"I've enjoyed working with you, and I hope we get to do many more projects together," he said, smiling. Then, he handed over his business card. "If you ever decide that you want to try consulting, give me a call."

I felt ready to take on a consulting role where I could mentor great, positive transformations. I reached out, interviewed, and secured a consultant position at Health Evolutions. A new chapter in Indianapolis was about to begin—and it would be my most exciting one yet, not to mention my most challenging.

Chapter FOUR
Cornfield to Heart Hospital

When I received my offer letter from Health Evolutions, I sold my house and packed my bags. Abby (my Springer Spaniel at the time) and I hit the road, driving from Pensacola up to Indianapolis. But even before we could get into the car, Steve Thomas, the president of Health Evolutions, called me on my phone.

"When are you getting into town?" he asked.

"Well, I'm driving up this weekend, so Monday morning," I said.

"Okay, good. We have a meeting on Monday morning at Hall, Render, Killian, Heath, & Lyman, and I want you there with me."

I spent my first day at Health Evolutions in an impressive boardroom on the 25th floor, looking out of the huge, wall-to-wall glass windows at the sunrise and sprawling Indianapolis below me. It was seven in the morning, and I sat in the boardroom of one of the largest healthcare law firms in the country with Vince Caponi, the market leader for the Indiana region, and Deeni Taylor, the chief strategy officer from St. Vincent Hospital, a full-service hospital in Indiana.

As the meeting began, two matters were established almost immediately. One, we needed someone to serve as the owner rep for St. Vincent and support the organization in its quest to build a freestanding heart hospital. Two, we would put out an offer to the physicians' group, which sought to build its own cardiac care center.

Here was the main challenge: the physicians' group had already received an offer from another healthcare organization but had signed a 90-day NDA that prohibited them from disclosing any other negotiations. Due to the NDA, we didn't even know the names of these organizations! But the 90-day NDA meant we had 45 days to put together a counteroffer that would please all 110 physician investors and, more importantly, blow the other offer out of the water.

After a few more meetings, it was decided that I would be the rep for St. Vincent. I was just getting started on the job, and I was already diving in deep. Clearly, I was in the right seat: everything was moving fast, and I was in the thick of it. I set to work.

Doug Dorrell, the director of finance at St. Vincent, and I spent hours and hours crunching numbers and reviewing financials, working at least 12 to 16 hours every day, even on the weekends. To say the least, we were burning the candle at both ends trying to put together the best counter proposal we could to create a win-win situation for everyone involved. As soon as we presented the end proposal to our senior leadership group, I immediately started making plans with the developers, looking at the different properties we could acquire to build the hospital, and narrowing down a couple of great options. Then, we engaged the developer, Bremner Real Estate; builders, Brasfield & Gorrie; and a large healthcare architectural firm, Earl Swensson Associates. They were all critical to the success of the project.

Within a week or so, the two architects from Earl Swensson and I completed a draft of the building to be presented along with the offer. Never before had a project been completed so quickly, and I owe it all to one special circumstance: there was nobody else on the design team to argue with me. I never operate in such a solo environment nor do I recommend it, but in this particular instance where time was of the essence, it sure came in handy that I was the only one working with the architects. Without much external input, I based the initial design on my years of experience working in different hospitals and in cardiology specifically. Then, with all these drafts ready, Karen Porter, a consulting colleague at Health Evolutions, took over. She put together different elements of the proposal—financials, plans, architectural designs, and timelines—and refined them into a solid binder that could be presented to the physicians' group.

Then came the day of the "ultimate meeting." (It felt so much bigger than all of us.) Every physician investor assembled in an auditorium and watched as we presented our offer. So much work had been put in by the whole team, and a lot was riding on the investors' decisions. Soon, the moment of truth arrived . . . and all 110 physician investors accepted our proposal. *Unanimously.*

Later, we'd find out that our rates came in less than a few dollars per square foot below what the other organization had planned, *and* we offered a 50-50 partnership for the physicians and St. Vincent to boot, unlike the other organization which wanted to own the majority of the shares. Not to mention, one of their former CEOs intended to build a separate, post-surgery recovery area, which just seemed to add yet another step to the patient's throughput and an unnecessary budget expense. We had already decided to make every bed in the hospital a critical care bed, so why not allow the patient to go straight from surgery to their bed and discharge them there rather than move them? Ultimately, it was these sizable differences and our plan's attention to detail that sealed the deal for St. Vincent. The physicians' group (which we later found out was the Care Group, the largest cardiology group in the nation at the time), signed an agreement with us, and we set down our pens and picked up our tools.

It was time to start building the Heart Center of Indiana.

We strategized on how to turn the property, a simple cornfield, into one of the nation's top cardiac care hospitals. It was exactly as difficult as it sounds. We discussed every single detail of the architectural plan, from whether or not we should put in deep footers to the colors of the building to the elevators. And this time, the physicians and board members could supply their thoughts, ideas, and feedback. Finally, I could operate according to the leadership values that I held in high regard.

The importance of having physicians involved in the process always remained at the forefront of my mind. After all, these would be the people working in the hospital day in and day out. Understanding and serving the needs of your staff comes first in servant leadership, and we made sure to include them in every single decision. This paid off in a major way.

I was of the opinion that in one of our facilities, two or three hand-washing stations for every 18 beds was more than adequate. In most hospitals that I had worked in so far, that had been the norm. Lana Lehman, a nurse by background who served on the board of directors, insisted that we had a handwashing station for every single bed. At the time, this felt unnecessary to me, and I just couldn't understand where she was coming from. But because I had faith in her judgment, I gave in and we followed Lana's plans. I'm glad we gave her full reign because it ended up being the right decision, especially when, years down the line, COVID reared its head and all those sinks made an enormous difference.

Fine-tuning the architectural plans made me think deeply about what most hospitals lacked that we could better implement. Two major improvement areas came to mind: the size of the operating rooms and the elevators.

The architects put standard-sized operating rooms in the plans, but I had been in enough of those to know they were not nearly big enough to accommodate all the necessary equipment, especially when working with robotic surgery. The elevators also had to be a certain size to ensure beds could easily roll into them and ease the movement of patients as much as possible—the cardiology surgeons pushed for this, and I was in complete agreement. The builders and architects all commented that they'd never put in an elevator the size of ours, a feat that could hold 20 people, but we all recognized it as essential and made it happen.

Even if the architects saw the logic in my arguments, one significant constraint hindered our efforts: budget. Every time you increase square footage, you also increase costs. But we couldn't talk our way out of these particular expenses. They would drastically improve the quality of care and efficiency we provided. Finally, after enough discussion and long hours of talking in circles, they let me have my way. And now, it is this infrastructure that has contributed to the success and reputation of the heart hospital. The Heart Center of Indiana, which would later be known as the St. Vincent Heart Center, had among the lowest costs of any hospital in the country and entered the top fifth percentile in patient and physician satisfaction.

To think we could have risked it all just to save a few thousand dollars!

BETTER THAN A HOTEL

Our determination to be intentional about quality and safety wasn't limited to the architectural design alone. We were laser-focused on building the culture of the hospital from the ground up as well. When we first began discussing the culture of the heart hospital, I posed the work group a question I had been pondering for a while: "Isn't it sad that you can stay at a Holiday Inn for $200 and get better service than when you pay thousands of dollars per day in a hospital?"

No one had an answer, but everyone agreed. We needed to refine and elevate some of these fundamental services, and we had to start talking about culture more intentionally. We began to make a few changes, such as calling our patients "guests" and patients' rooms "guest suites." (When we started to hire and train associates, we never referred to them as "employees" but instead called them "team members." Along the same lines, we didn't have directors; we had "team leaders.") A trained chef also designed our cafeteria's menus, meaning that the menu changed monthly and was available to guests at any time. In fact, people would come to our hospital just to eat because the food was better than many of the restaurants in the area! *That's* quality. *That's* thoughtfully catering to the needs of the patients so they feel cared for. We built the entire culture of the hospital on the foundation of servant leadership and trained all our team members to operate based on these values. Our culture was palatable.

The main justification for raising the bar on customer service (apart from providing comfort) was that in order to survive in the market and outdo our competitors, we needed to achieve a low-cost, high-satisfaction model.

Dr. Bill Storer, the chief medical officer, supported this idea and said, "This should be a no-brainer. If you have high-quality care, it should inherently be low-cost because fewer mistakes are made. By making the best decisions, we can maximize the outcomes." We built this culture of quality, safety, and exceptional customer service from its basic concept to execution and training. As you already know, mission, vision, and values are a few of my deepest passions, and building these up in the heart hospital from scratch felt incredibly fulfilling.

The Heart Center of Indiana opened its doors on December 2, 2002.

Once the hospital hired its official CEO, my work was done. I decided that it was time to move away and let the new CEO assume his role and responsibilities. After pulling in all those late nights and long hours, I decided to take a quick sabbatical and relax, so I, of course, went to one of the most beautifully tranquil places in the world: Wine Country, California. There, I helped out two of my friends who had just started to build a gourmet deli and wine shop. I got to know many winemakers, eat plenty of delicious food, and decompress for long, long hours.

One day, while helping out my friends at the deli during the rush season, I received a phone call from Deeni Taylor and Steve Thomas.

"John, we're in trouble," they told me.

The heart hospital had encountered some financial dilemmas and undergone a leadership change. Deeni and Steve wanted me to serve as the interim CEO until a permanent replacement could be recruited. Of course, at the time, I could say nothing but yes. After all, I helped develop the cardiac center from the ground up. How could I turn away from the relationships I formed there? How could I say no to such a critical mission, not to mention a mission that I helped create?

Knowing my answer, I cut my sabbatical short and moved back to Indianapolis with the idea of serving for maybe a couple of months, six months at most if they really struggled to find a qualified CEO. Little did I know, I would end up serving for six years instead. And that by the end of my term, St. Vincent would grow into one of the largest cardiology programs in the nation.

Chapter FIVE
Rolling Up My Sleeves

"I'm not going to stand here and tell you to trust and respect me," I said to the leadership team. "It's not something I can demand. But I do want to tell you that we can work together and turn this hospital around in six months."

I looked around the room at their faces—some nodded appreciatively and others looked skeptical. Dr. Richard Fogel, the chairman of the board for the Heart Center, had been kind enough to give me this opportunity to meet with everyone and introduce myself as the new interim CEO. I wanted to make sure that no one would leave the room without at least knowing a thing or two about me. I hoped to establish a rapport, even if it was a subtle one, so they could freely approach me with any questions or problems later on. So, I said a few more things about myself: my experience in the healthcare industry so far, my role in helping start and build the Heart Center, and the values of servant leadership that I hold close to my heart. I also told them that I deeply valued their opinions; after all, they were here for the first year when I wasn't, which surely let them observe and take note of what was working and, most importantly, what wasn't.

"The board has already told me about some challenging areas and issues that need to be handled, but I'd like input from all of you to perform a SWOT analysis and understand exactly what our strengths, weaknesses, opportunities, and threats are," I continued. "With a consensus about our top priorities, we can strategize and move forward together."

I knew it would be hard to gain the trust of the leadership team that had just lost faith due to the actions of my predecessor. The old CEO would often put on scrubs and sit with the nurses on the floor, which only made it that much harder to keep things straight, and the ex-CFO had created major financial performance issues. But I knew I couldn't get anywhere alone—I needed the leadership team on my side and ready to take initiative. We needed to work together to energize the Heart Center with a common mission and vision. With those in hand, we could turn the tide.

By the time the meeting ended, we had a list of initiatives we wanted to accomplish, and to me, that was already a sign of a well-done meeting. But then, when a few members came up to me as everyone exited the room, I was presented with even more proof.

"It's so refreshing to have you lead the room because you know what you're talking about. It might seem too early, but we already feel a lot more comfortable with you at the helm," they said. To say the least, my very first meeting with the team was incredibly affirming. I looked forward to keeping the trust and respect I had already gained and proving that I would work hard for them.

I immediately sat down in my office and started going over the revenue and expense reports. In the meeting, I declared that it was not enough to simply focus on expense reduction; we also needed to spend equal time on growth and revenue. However, it was understandable why the board and the leadership team wanted to be on the defensive—they had ended the past year in the red.

To be exact, nearly *one million dollars in the red*.

It was time for me to do my homework and collaborate with my team to come up with a strategy that could help the Heart Center thrive without draining all our resources. We were in damage control mode, but that was no reason for us to shy away from implementing new programs that could help us grow.

I reminded my team that the ratio of impact on the bottom line between expense and revenue is one to three. So, if we channeled most of our efforts into revenue management and improvement, that would make up for a few errors on the expense side. With that in mind, we revamped the revenue cycle and improved our coding in the medical records. That move saw immediate results, and our revenue started to improve within 30 days. Now, it was time to turn toward expenses—except we uncovered more than just a few errors taking place in the dark.

BUILDING STRUCTURE—AND TRUST

To put it bluntly, a lot of finger-pointing went around.

A German healthcare solutions and services company, Siemens Medical, handled everything from billing to imaging and equipment to our phone and information systems. In essence, they had a hand in every critical part of our daily operations. However, Siemens slowly lost its grip on billing and coding, and without understanding that the Heart Center was responsible for some of the workload and accountability, my predecessors resorted to the blame game. As I discovered early on in my career, criticism and accusations tend to worsen, not solve, problems. What Siemens needed was support and accountability to ensure their side ran smoothly. In my effort to strategize a plan for moving forward, I immediately got in touch with their executives.

I understood that while we might have outsourced a part of operations to Siemens, it was ultimately our responsibility to notice and fix discrepancies. At times like these, I was grateful that I *breathed* billing and coding, thanks to my experience at

O'Connor (as the cardiac service line administrator), Sacred Heart (with Brenda Erner and the Daughters of Charity National Cardiac Database), and with the Indiana Heart Institute. The executives at Siemens and I put our heads together, broke down the problem into process steps, developed a dashboard to monitor ourselves and the metrics, and renegotiated some contracts to pave the way for solutions and results to stream in.

A brunt of these tasks was performed by the revenue cycle management work group I put together in conjunction with Siemens. That soon put us on the right track, and the Heart Center began chugging along without issue.

I also formed an expense reduction work group and a marketing and development work group, and all three of these committees kept pushing out initiatives and smoothing out all the creases. We were on a scheduled timeline where we met every two weeks, debriefed, planned, and implemented. Within 90 days, we turned around the financials of the organization. Dr. Fogel and the board were beyond amazed, and I was incredibly proud of the various teams that had worked together with so much dedication. We made something incredible happen every single day, and it was fulfilling to work with teams that were as passionate about the Heart Center as I was.

Physician leadership takes a huge chunk of the credit for turning around the Heart Center. My duty in all of this was to scaffold their ideas with tools and support so they could freely implement as they wished.

One of those areas was the matter of adding more beds. There was space for it—the second floor had 40 beds, the third floor had 20 beds with the shell space to fit in another 20, and the fourth floor had enough space for an additional 80 beds. We built the hospital this way to give us the option to expand if necessary. However, a clause was built into the contract at the very beginning when St. Vincent signed with the Care Group: in order to build out 20 additional beds, the Heart Center had to run at an occupancy rate greater than 85 percent for a rolling six months in a row. St. Vincent added that into the contract because they were afraid the doctors would move their patients from the St. Vincent hospital to the Heart Center, which was only 10 minutes away. They hoped that by putting in a difficult-to-attain clause, they would have a better chance of retaining healthy volumes.

But they failed to account for one thing: our incredible team.

I heard the needs of the physicians, and together, we created a program that would send out an email alert to key physicians and the leadership of the Care Group when our patient volume sank below 85 percent.

That way, they could call in patients and accommodate some space for them. This email alert would go out daily and made it much easier to mobilize a collective effort to exceed the occupancy number for six months in a row.

It was as wild as it sounds—we even had to pull in patients from ambulatory care and emergency services some days! However, it was all worth it when the daily census and numbers were presented six months later. Most of this growth came from patients who would have gone to our competitors when we had no beds. St. Vincent could find no standing to withhold approval. We could build out the beds we needed, which then launched us forward like never before.

BIG "O" AND LITTLE "O"

Within the six months that I served as the interim CEO, the Heart Center edged out of its downward trend in revenue and entered the green. We went up and up, and the physicians and board were beyond happy. Initially, when the Heart Center was formed, St. Vincent and the Care Group wanted a 50-50 ownership, so the physicians could have equal control in the decision-making processes and operations, especially because these decisions affected *them* the most. Now, with their input in leadership combined with all the initiatives we had taken toward explosive revenue growth and reduced expenses, the situation was brighter than ever for the physicians. They felt a sense of responsibility and pride in their hospital that was long overdue.

This is what Dr. Fogel often called the big "O" and the little "o." The big "O" referred to the ownership of the place as a whole and working toward making it the best possible, and the little "o" referenced financial ownership and the physicians getting their due when the hospital performed better.

While it might seem like the unquestionably best idea for physicians to invest (at the time, physician-owned hospitals had not been legislatively prevented yet), there was a risk: the minimum investment was a significant amount to ask physicians to stake. If the hospital performed poorly, they would not only lose their influence but also their investments. I personally knew a physician who had a lot of anxiety about putting up so much of his funds. In fact, he felt so nervous about it that he went around taking a poll of how safe we all thought the investment would be! Now, when I see him around, I ask, "Hey, how's that investment going?" I get a broad smile in return every time.

During these past months, they paid Health Evolutions a considerable amount for me—I was still technically serving in this role as a "consultant." But as I was soon coming up on my contract terms, the board asked Dr. Fogel to form a CEO recruitment committee to search for a permanent CEO. Weeks passed, and nothing changed.

Suddenly, I realized something.

I went up to Dr. Fogel and asked, "What's going on? You haven't even started the search committee, and you're paying me so much more than you should. Something isn't adding up."

It was then that he shut the door, sat down across from me, knit his fingers, and asked, "John, what's it going to take?"

I blinked.

"Name your price," he said before I could talk. "We don't want another CEO—we want *you*."

I was flattered. And I understood where he was coming from. However, I was going through an internal conflict myself and needed time to detangle. I asked him to give me 48 hours to think about it and left the room. I immediately wrote down my thoughts and made a list of sorts. No consultant had ever left Steve Thomas at Health Evolutions. I would be the first if I resigned. An intimidating thought. I set up a lunch date with him so I could discuss the offer, my thoughts, and his opinion about it.

When I told Steve what Dr. Fogel said, he was shocked but recovered quickly.

"Just so you know, you have St. Vincent on one side and physician investors on the other," he said. "If you're fine with having your balls squeezed by both these owner groups, then I'm not going to stand in your way."

That sure was one way to think about it. However, I chose to instead focus on the fact that Steve had just given me the green light, and at some point in the past 48 hours, I had already made my decision as well.

So, I told Dr. Fogel that I had a couple of requirements. I needed both owner groups to agree that I was the right person for the job, and I didn't want to go through a formal search process as it would be a waste of time for me, the other candidates, and the hiring committee. I met with both owner groups personally and received each of their approvals, and the board granted me my second request as well. Before I knew it, we drew up an employment agreement.

I was now the permanent CEO of the Heart Center of Indiana, an organization I helped start, build, and now lead. I felt like I was in the very place I needed to be, and I would stay right there for the next six years.

Chapter SIX
Where Corn Don't Grow

L. H. Bailey, the vice chair around the time I became the full-time CEO at the Heart Center, was one of the people who interviewed me as a formality. He had a commanding presence—if he walked into a restaurant, everyone practically bowed. He was the type of person who would tell a waiter exactly how he wanted his eggs done and, if he had the option, probably would've picked out the eggs he wanted himself.

I only bring up eggs because he interviewed me over breakfast at the Comfort Inn. My order was simple: an omelet. To this day, L. H. Bailey loves telling people at the Heart Center this story: "What most of you don't know is that John Stewart was not an easy get for us. But I was able to get him for the small price of a three-egg omelet."

Breakfast aside, my six-year tenure as the CEO of the Heart Center was full of invaluable moments, relationships, and success stories, and I owe it all to the wonderful team of physicians, nurses, and administrators who dedicated themselves to superior service every single day. When I think of how far I had come, I'm always reminded of the song "Where Corn Don't Grow" by Travis Tritt. I had gone out into the world and taken on the challenge, leaving behind the farmlands of small-town Kentucky I had known so well. But while I was far from home, in a place where corn don't grow, I was living the life I had dreamed of—one where I could serve those who served others.

While I could write an entire book about everything I've done, learned, and gained during this time, I'll instead try to distill six years of insights into a single chapter. Think of this as a textbook of sorts; I'll share key changes we made in the organization to improve service, financials, and culture while also going over the processes we engaged in to implement them and see success. Let's begin with one of my core passions: the mission, vision, and values of an organization.

A FOCUS ON QUALITY

While the Heart Center was only a year old, St. Vincent was a long-established organization. It already had hundreds of years' worth of mission, vision, and values developed and in place in its various subsidiaries. However, the Heart Center wasn't wholly St. Vincent's; it was a 50-50 joint venture, and as such, it couldn't simply absorb the culture of its parent company. It had to find and build its own.

This topic came up when I was involved in the building of the Heart Center in a consultant role. At the time, I declined any part in forming the mission, vision, and values. I believed that the one leading the organization, the to-be CEO, should have been given the opportunity to lead this process with the board. After all, I didn't plan on staying after the Heart Center opened its doors, so it wasn't my place to dictate the culture of the organization if I wasn't around to observe the daily operations.

By the time I stepped into the CEO role at the Heart Center of Indiana, the prior CEO and my predecessors already had the mission, vision, and values of the organization well established. This is one of the initiatives I give them full credit for. They channeled appropriate time, energy, and resources toward developing these three elements and integrating them into the heart of the organization. They had the right priority in mind when they built the Heart Center around one core value: providing the highest level of care. The mission, vision, and values they established went on to serve the organization for six years before it eventually merged to form the St. Vincent Heart Center and St. Vincent Medical Group (which I discuss in more detail in chapter seven).

However, I did notice one negative cultural trait: the leadership team had a tough time accepting change. Just the thought of implementing a few changes to their operations caused them so much stress that they would burst into tears. I remember sharing my surprise with Dr. Fogel when conversations ended with tense nerves and hurt feelings when I'd only been communicating how to improve certain areas of the Heart Center. Later on, I found out that a lot of this stress was caused by the financial issues my predecessors created, and thankfully, untangling that dilemma enabled my team to take charge and adopt a more positive attitude toward change.

One of these significant changes was our treatment process for heart attacks. Remember the work we did at Sacred Heart to build a chest pain center specifically to improve our response time and treatment of heart attacks? Well, this time around at the Heart Center, my team and I found a way to elevate care even more, and it helped that we had a much bigger and better infrastructure in place to facilitate this growth.

We realized that our balloon time (which is tracked from the minute a patient passes through our door until the time they get to the cath lab and the angioplasty balloon is inflated) was too long, and if we wanted to improve our treatment, we needed to improve our protocols first. So, we worked with various suburban hospitals and teams to advance these protocols, and we upscaled our chest pain management too. While this was hard work and resulted in many changes to the way things had been done before, we fully embraced the transformation as a team. We had our eyes trained on our mission of providing quality care, and this propelled us to evolve our existing processes and systems.

Our research and development department was another notable team that formed the core of our mission, vision, and values. We were a leading institution in the country on the research and development of new procedures and drugs, especially in the cardiology space. Not to mention, at one point, we had five physician leaders who led national organizations across the country. One of our proudest accomplishments was that the Heart Center was one of the first in the nation to have a hybrid operating room, and we were a leader in performing minimally invasive bypass surgery. With each new program, initiative, and department, we grew as an institution and lived our mission, vision, and values to the fullest extent.

Nobody executed our values better than our physician leaders. The Heart Center was initially created with a very important goal in mind: to empower physicians in the decision-making and leading of the organization. That's why they held half of the stake in the company. So, throughout the six years I served as CEO, my main objective was to provide physicians with the support they needed to take the lead on everything. And Dr. Fogel was one of the most active and involved chairmen of a board I had ever seen. We referred to him as the Energizer Bunny because, once someone presented a potential solution or change to him, he would champion it and drive resources toward making it happen. When Dr. Fogel became involved in something, it was guaranteed to be a success. He had just as much of a focus on the upkeep of our mission, vision, and values as I did and consequently acted as an excellent resource for any physician leader who wanted to start an initiative that directly aligned with those values. It was this shared vision and drive that propelled the Heart Center to embrace quality care and hospitality like no one else. We achieved patient, employee, *and* stakeholder satisfaction—day in and day out.

EXPENSE REDUCTION: THE 80/20 RULE

When I started as interim CEO, the Heart Center was in the red. With tensions running high, the board and leadership teams looked to cut expenses—significantly and fast. We immediately started by prioritizing each line item in the expense budget, starting with our most expensive items and renegotiating those.

One of these expenses was our largest vendor, which we had to ask to forego the multimillion dollars we owed them, and then we had to perform a similar evaluation and renegotiation with all our large vendors. This goes without saying, but they weren't too happy about that. However, I reassured them that by continuing to do business with us, there would be much better prospects on the horizon as we began to scale and expand.

Part of prioritizing meant that we also had to take a close look at staffing and reevaluate the productivity standards for every unit and process area (i.e. our departments). One of the big changes we had to make here was tweaking our care delivery model, right-sizing our staff by eliminating travel nurse positions and bringing security in-house, and combining the positions of COO and CNO to create a new one that would take on both responsibilities. These were some of the giant, actionable strategies we were able to put into place by following the 80/20 rule, which recommends focusing on the 20 percent of your items that account for 80 percent of your total expense.

Of course, other changes needed to be made, one of which was particularly hard on most of our staff: we had to downsize our coffee machines.

When my predecessors introduced high-tech, expensive, gourmet latte machines in every single unit within the building, they must've been in a real carte blanche mood. These machines had a significantly negative impact on our budget, so the CFO and I said we should cut them. People were so upset by this decision that I had to bring in the entire leadership team, take a stand, and say, "Folks, we need a healthy dose of reality here. Do you want expensive coffee, or do you want the right amount of staff?" Finally, that ended up introducing some perspective into the situation. Also, I'm sure it helped that I ultimately compromised and agreed to keep one machine in the cafeteria and one in the doctor's lounge. All other units still had coffee—they just weren't foamy vanilla cappuccinos!

Expense reduction was also a priority in terms of equipment, though this was a complex problem as most hospitals find themselves in a tricky battle with physicians when attempting to buy less expensive devices and medications. However, this was one of those instances when physician ownership really came into play for the Heart Center. In cardiology, equipment and medications can be extremely expensive, but when a physician spends their own money as an investment into the company, they take the side of leadership when it comes to cutting costs. Remember the big "O" and little "o" we talked about? This is where the financial ownership element came into effect, allowing physicians to make carefully vetted decisions from both a quality and fiscal standpoint. As a result, our physicians were more than willing to purchase equipment that had lower costs as long as it didn't negatively impact the quality of patient care. We could slash down our supplies and pharmacy expenses under the guidance of physicians who could make effective decisions on what was absolutely necessary for providing quality care and what we could justifiably cut back on.

But expense reduction is not just about slashing down expenses. Some expenses are necessary to boost revenue. In order to improve our finances, we had to spend our budget on two initiatives: appointing a clinical PharmD to every unit and retaining our partnership with the Indiana Heart Institute (now called Navion). Hiring a clinical PharmD for every department is not an expense most hospitals would even consider, but I knew it could prove to be invaluable. And I was right. Within six months of implementation, this initiative had not only paid for itself but demonstrated how it could dramatically reduce overall drug expenses. Many hospitals wouldn't do this, but I'm glad we did. These pharmacists acted as critical resources for physicians and nurses in every unit, allowing the leadership team to cut back on unnecessary expenses and simultaneously increase the quality of care. A win-win.

At the Heart Center, I had time and again managed to prove to the leadership team and the physicians that Navion was an incredible resource for us—their data analysis and management systems helped us in our research efforts, operation improvement strategies, and better understanding the care and treatments we provided. However, I had to fight many a battle with those who didn't come from clinical backgrounds and couldn't see the value in the data Navion provided. Later on, when I served as the president of St. Vincent Medical Group, I would attend St. Vincent Health committee meetings. Every time, the regional CEOs brought up Navion and how they wanted to cut the program. I knew physicians found Navion extremely helpful, and consequently, we would descend into heated arguments right there. After all, for people who didn't understand the real value of this, it was a pretty big line item on our expense budget and one they thought we could easily eliminate with no significant impact.

Now, the success of Navion is proof enough of its value; the vision of Brenda Erner, the vice president of data management at Navion, and I had been realized. When I was at Sacred Heart, I had the opportunity to work with Brenda on the Daughters of Charity National Cardiac Database, and over my time at the Heart Center and later at St. Vincent Medical Group, we worked in partnership yet again. I suppose you could say that my admiration, respect, and trust in Brenda and her organization runs deep. And it definitely helped that Navion was doing exceptional work on every project.

When Ascension announced they were considering selling Navion to a third party, physicians rose up in support and demonstrated the importance of Navion's work to them and their hospitals. It was this loud backing that urged healthcare organizations to reconsider and see Navion for what it was—a diamond in the rough. As of 2023, Navion is doing data abstraction for the entire Ascension organization across the board, along with serving many other healthcare organizations. The value of data abstraction has finally entered the public consensus, and with each passing day, hospitals and physicians embrace and leverage its value. It's a pleasure to see how far Navion has come, and I'm grateful that I could support Brenda and her trusty band of amazing individuals—Kevin Willmann, Tom Lane, and countless board members and physicians—in achieving the goals and vision they set for themselves.

REVENUE ENHANCEMENT: NEVER SAY NO TO A TRANSFER

Just as we had kick-started expense reduction initiatives, I also knew we needed to start improving our revenue if we wanted to quickly turn around our financials. This process included renegotiating certain payer contracts as well as evaluating the revenue cycle, which had to do with enhancing our billing and coding systems. As I discussed in the last chapter, improving the revenue cycle meant fostering shared accountability and partnership with Siemens and Navion to make operations and financial processes a lot more efficient.

Whenever the right course of action seemed like an impossible task, we found a way to make it possible.

When I first started at the Heart Center, I noticed that before performing surgery, the doctors would come to me at times and ask if the insurance would pay for it. Taken aback, I started asking questions, and soon, I found out that the physicians were instructed by the ex-CFO to first check if the hospital was going to be reimbursed or not before providing treatment.

I was shocked and dismayed. But now that the flawed reasoning had been brought to light, we were able to reverse this entire culture together. We reinforced that physicians know best and need to always, *always* do what's right for the patient—and to leave matters of insurance and reimbursement for the leadership team to handle. With this new change, Dr. Storer and I began to set up contact with insurance agencies and find a way to reverse any denial decisions.

I wholeheartedly believe that insurance companies shouldn't even be involved in these decisions as their motives are often skewed from the get-go. By delaying a reimbursement, they are able to continue monetizing from the generated interest. Knowing this, Dr. Storer and I were relentless. We challenged every single denial and kept challenging until they reversed the decision. It didn't take them long to realize that they would not be able to win against Dr. Storer, a board-certified cardiologist. By aggressively pursuing denials, we were able to get the reimbursements we were owed—in fact, within three months of fighting for every case, Dr. Storer had already brought enough cash flow into the hospital to cover his annual salary! Most hospitals would've just written it off, but we were on a mission to provide the resources to enable our surgeons and cardiologists to do what they do best—heal patients.

A part of our revenue enhancement strategies also included a focus on growth and development. At the Heart Center, we had a saying: "Never say no to a transfer." If we wanted to grow and keep our numbers high, we could never turn away a patient. I'm not going to say everything was smooth sailing from here—quite the opposite actually. This made our jobs more difficult, but because our physicians and nurses were so committed to the idea, we achieved several considerable goals, including the rolling six-month challenge of retaining greater than 85 percent occupancy. This win helped us bring in more beds, more staff, and more revenue. We all went through those tough six months together and emerged victorious—and with that victory, we had the opportunity to throw a huge party to recognize everybody's efforts in helping the Heart Center grow so tremendously.

I cannot talk about expansion efforts without commending Beth Cisco. She was such an incredible vice president of marketing and development that when she began to single-handedly elevate the Heart Center's brand, we received recognition in all forms, including a prestigious award from Healthgrades, a leading online resource for comprehensive information about physicians and hospitals. But she didn't stop there. Beth took every award we won and used them in our marketing to enhance our brand even more. Suddenly, we had facts, numbers, and accolades that we could leverage in all of our marketing efforts. If that wasn't enough, she and her team also came up with some truly amazing campaigns.

In one campaign geared at marketing our cardiac services, a positioning line was developed based on a phrase I often said: "Is your heart in the right place?"

Beth's predominant mission was improving healthcare accessibility for all. It was a driving force in each of her campaigns, particularly when she decided to enter the hospital's float in the Pride parade. Unfortunately, in many cases within medical spaces, those who are part of the LGBT+ community, especially people of color, are often not treated with the same level of care as those not belonging to that community. Beth felt strongly about fostering inclusivity and presenting the Heart Center as a safe space for all—and she did all of this on her own. I only found out later, when my phone started buzzing with calls from everyone asking me about the float! It was a testament to Beth's leadership and ability to make things happen. She didn't even need to ask for permission; that's how brilliant her ideas were every time.

Beth is also known, even to this day, as the one responsible for ideating the Heart Center's incredible heart scan campaign. Wanting to pull in more people who did not yet have a relationship with a cardiologist, Beth considered multiple marketing channels but ultimately identified an opportunity with the Heart Center's heart scan offering. At the time, heart scans put patients back around $250 as an out-of-pocket fee. But Beth asked, "What if we could reduce that charge and pull in new patients who wouldn't be able to afford a scan otherwise?" We already had the staff and equipment in place. So, why not?

Doing so could inform participants sooner rather than later if they had any complications, meaning we could provide early intervention for them and register new patients.

Initially, we launched $99 heart scans, which turned out to be a hit, not to mention a major opportunity for us to expand and drive community impact. On one occasion, a team member's father even came in for a heart scan. He was in great shape and led an extremely active lifestyle, so anyone would think he'd have a perfect score. Turns out, he had such a high score and so much blockage that by Thursday, he required urgent open-heart surgery—all because of a $99 heart scan.

Over time, competing hospitals began to see the outstanding results from this initiative, so much so that many established their own similar campaigns. This led Beth into my office one day.

"John," she said. "We need to reduce ours to a $49 heart scan."

I blinked at her. "How are we going to accomplish that?"

"I've done all the research, and I've figured it out. Again, the staff is there, and the equipment is there. Why not do it?"

"Now, Beth, are you going to come into my office next week and ask for a $25 heart scan?"

She just laughed and said, "Let's start at $49."

The Heart Center still offers $49 heart scans to this day, in addition to the many hospitals across the state of Indiana that do as well. This became an intentional and strategic way for us to access new folks, yes, but more importantly . . . it was the right thing to do. And it continues to result in astonishing outcomes for both patients and the hospital.

After understanding her capacity for creativity, it should be no surprise that Beth brought another incredible campaign to the halls of the Heart Center: the Go Red for Women campaign started by the American Heart Association. This campaign focused on raising awareness of the risk of cardiovascular disease in women and empowering them to take charge of their heart health. Seeing the campaign as an opportunity to uplift another demographic that often faces disparity in healthcare, Beth wanted to market specifically to women in an effort to spread awareness and showcase the Heart Center. At the time, the Go Red for Women campaign was still in its beginning stages, but Beth took it and made it something so much bigger than anyone thought was possible. She set up the Heart Center to be its presenting sponsor and committed wholly to the cause—we all donned red ties and dresses at Go Red for Women events in addition to providing numerous heart health education and engagement offerings at these events. Beth even found a way to make our entire building light up red! Recognizing the success of Beth's efforts in taking the campaign to a whole other level, the American Heart Association asked her to serve on the national marketing committee and the regional board of directors, both of which she proudly accepted.

When we started airing TV commercials, Beth directed them all and even used our own doctors and nurses as the face of the hospital. And she was smart about it—she bought out ad slots that only targeted Indiana and not the entire country. Only later did my leadership team and I realize that she purposefully picked a time that coincided with the Superbowl! Imagine my surprise when I kept getting calls from excited physician investors telling me, "I just saw an ad about the Heart Center during the Superbowl!" Though, they would usually follow their first comment with concern: "How much did we pay for that?" I had the happy pleasure of telling them that Beth managed to pull this off at a fraction of the cost anyone would expect. I told you—she was incredible.

Beth Cisco

Strategic Marketing and Business Development Consultant, Former Vice President of Marketing and Development at the Heart Center of Indiana

John and I met at a relatively small management consulting firm, Health Evolutions. The three principals, two of whom are sadly no longer with us, had a talent for pulling together a group of distinctly unique individuals in terms of experience, intellect, and skill sets. Even with our different areas of expertise, the group had a few things in common: passion, a relentless drive to deliver high-quality results, a spirit of collaboration, and a commitment to doing the right work.

Health Evolutions was a client of mine at St. Claire Cisco Group, and Steve Thomas and Nathan Mowery courted me to come on board as a team member. Not only would I support the marketing efforts of Health Evolutions, but I would also serve as a branding and marketing consultant. The first client I had was the Heart Center of Indiana.

About six months into my consultative relationship with the Heart Center, L. H. Bailey, the chairman of the board at the time, took me out to lunch. Over a glass of white wine (his preference as I like red!), he asked if I would formally join the Heart Center as the vice president of marketing and development, which included anything and everything that touched the patients (or as we referred to them, "guests") and their respective family members. I served housekeeping, food services, scheduling, concierge staff, and marketing, and I also was, to a lesser degree, responsible for the heart emergency unit. An 80-bed hospital may appear to have a small footprint, but I felt honored to serve so many people in a myriad of functions, sometimes putting on scrubs or serving food at our cafe—any task needed to help the hospital make a difference.

A competitor, the Indiana Heart Hospital—also a specialty heart hospital—opened its doors a few months before the Heart Center of Indiana. The two brands merged in the eyes of the public, so much so that ambulances would often mix up the names and deliver patients to the wrong hospital. This made it imperative for our marketing team to ask sooner rather than later, "How can we elevate the Heart Center and our specific location?"

It was actually my voice that delivered the new moniker on our advertising campaign: "The Heart Center of Indiana at 106th & N. Meridian." This simple line established a geographical touchpoint, so everyone, from patients to EMS, knew that the Heart Center was a freestanding, independent heart hospital. Heart care was our bailiwick and singular focus—this is what we did each and every day.

In addition, we worked closely with Healthgrades, an organization that tracked our performance and quality outcomes from a data standpoint. As a marketer, I have always appreciated the concreteness of data since, as a principle, you never want to arbitrarily label your organization as "the best" without objective proof to back it up. Healthgrades tracked such data in three-year increments, meaning that any complications specific to conditions and procedures would impact the organization's ratings for a rolling three years. The Heart Center, as a whole, was attentive and intentional about ensuring that our physicians, surgeons, clinical support staff, and others were in lockstep. We had to provide and deliver the best care at every moment.

So, when Healthgrades distinguished us as the number-one program in Indiana based on irrefutable data, the marketing team pounced on the opportunity—how would we make certain everyone knew that we achieved this distinctive and distinguished position?

We needed to develop a campaign that was definitive, declarative, and simple but not braggadocious or arrogant. A basic objective of marketing is to make the message digestible so the audience can quickly understand it and then use data to support your claim. With data not only from Healthgrades but also from our patient experience results, we created a positioning line that read, "The best heart care in Indiana. Period." This became a rallying statement that spoke to our current and prospective patients and also to the retention and acquisition of top talent, no matter if we needed a new housekeeper or surgeon.

I strive to plan initiatives and marketing campaigns that surprise people and stand out from the noise—especially considering that Central Indiana is one of the most competitive areas in the US for healthcare. John, being my colleague since our time at Health Evolutions, understood my brain and intentions. He leads from the heart *and* the head. When I would come to him with marketing-related ideas, he would rarely challenge my thinking. Given his level of respect and support for our team, he'd much more frequently nod and say, "I trust you implicitly. Let's do this."

I get emotional thinking about one campaign in particular: the Go Red for Women movement. I remember the meeting I had in the fall of 2003 with two members of the local American Heart Association to specifically discuss Go Red for Women. This campaign was just being launched, and Indianapolis was one of the first local markets across the US. Though the American Heart Association had already presented it to two other hospital systems, I told them, "I want this. I want this for the Heart Center."

The Heart Center of Indiana became the proud presenting sponsor of Go Red for Women in Central Indiana, an initiative that has grown exponentially over the years due to the hard work put in by those at the American Heart Association and its respective sponsors, community partners, and volunteers. The nonprofit raises awareness of the clinical care gaps involved in women's greatest health threat, cardiovascular disease, as nearly 45 percent of women over the age of 20 are living with some form of it.[4] With the partnership between the Heart Center and Go Red for Women, more women in our community became knowledgeable and proactive about their own health—a mission I'm both proud and honored we contributed to as an organization.

Playing to the mission, vision, and values of the Heart Center, why wouldn't we participate in initiatives like the Go Red for Women campaign? Why wouldn't we invest a percent of our marketing budget if it meant informing women of symptoms, risks, and threats associated with cardiovascular disease? And why wouldn't we, for the month of February, even have our *building* go red? These were my thoughts as I approached the head of facilities, who, much like myself, often has an irreverent voice.

"I'm not making our building red, Beth. Not for you. Not for anyone," he told me.

"We're the Heart Center of Indiana, the presenting sponsor for Go Red for Women," I said. "I've looked into it. We can use inexpensive gels to change the colors of the outside lights, and it wouldn't be much work for your team."

Still, he denied my request.

It was then I learned that he liked Crown Royal whiskey.

Days later, I approached him in a hallway, a purple bag in hand. Our building went red after that. To this day, it goes red for the month of February. (And the head of facilities and I still like to tell this story, 20 years later!)

Even though my role was not clinically oriented, I still approached my profession as a marketer knowing our team could make a real impact and change the lives of those we served. John, as a true visionary, also understood this—the Heart Center of Indiana was like no other hospital of its kind. We had to ensure we were viable, relevant, and part of the narrative. With pride in physician ownership and our partnerships with St. Vincent Health and various community organizations, our incredible team, empowered and ignited by John's skill in servant leadership, felt called to our work and made a lasting impact as a result. We wanted to create a resource that would endure, with excellence, for 20, 50, 100 years, and thanks to many brilliant hands and minds, we delivered the best heart care in Indiana. Period.

Through the combined impact of an improved revenue cycle, expansion strategies, and unbeatable marketing campaigns, the Heart Center saw hockey stick growth. This opened us up for new opportunities, partnerships, and transformation during the six years I served as the CEO. Our revenue enhancement and expense reduction committees had outdone themselves—the Heart Center was out of the red and gaining speed as it launched upward. As I like to say, we were on like gangbusters!

PHILOSOPHIES ON LEADERSHIP

Throughout my career, I've operated on a set of personal philosophies that I think deserve all the credit. Without these principles to guide me, I'm not sure how successfully I would have executed my personal mission, vision, and values in everything that I do.

One of these philosophies was introduced to me by none other than Lana Lehman. Lana Lehman had served as the executive vice president of the Care Group and a board member of the Heart Center. At the very beginning, when we were still developing and building the Heart Center, we interviewed three different companies that specialized in cardiovascular imaging to supply our equipment, which is when we decided to work with Siemens. One time, Lana and I flew out to their headquarters in Germany for a partnership meeting. Afterward, while sitting in a pub and discussing the Heart Center, Lana said something that stuck with me from that moment onward: "Remember, John, it's *always* about the doctors."

If you're an executive of an organization with various leadership teams, you know that any decision requires input from multiple people. However, in the case of healthcare organizations, no opinions are as important as the physicians' opinions. Even before hearing Lana put it into words, I always based every transformative decision on this one rule, never moving ahead until I consulted with doctors first. By doing so, I empowered them to lead, made changes that streamlined their jobs, and most importantly, got out of their way.

During my term as interim CEO, people often came up to me to ask how I managed 110 physicians every day. My answer was always, "I don't."

Physicians already know the best protocols and operations, so my role as a leader was to simply provide support and individual development where needed. When you work with physicians as closely as I have, you pick up on certain ways of communication. An approach I recommend is utilizing data. Data is objective . . . and physicians never want to perform one or two standard deviations below the norm of their peers. Despite this, they might still counter your data with two arguments, either saying, "Your data is flawed," or "My patients are sicker."

The best way to counter the first argument is to use abstracted data, which is much more accurate than the charge data hospitals typically use. Charge data is documented by physicians in the medical record when there's a charged procedure. The biggest problem with this type of data is that many hospitals fail to maintain accuracy and update it frequently enough, and soon, the charges are no longer concurrent with actual practice. This data then needs to be coded and later converted into a bill—all complex processes that make it hard for hospitals to maintain the data effectively. On the other hand, abstracted data is coded directly from the practice and reviewed by RNs trained in extracting and reading it, making this data comparatively more accurate and up-to-date. It's specifically for abstracted data that we partnered with Navion.

For the second argument ("my patients are sicker"), it's essential to gently remind the physician that their patients have about the same acuity, or severity of illness, as other patients. It's not uncommon for many physicians to become emotionally invested in their patients and report their symptoms as unusually bad, so a reminder helps them view the data without bias. Once you work through these two arguments with them, then physicians will be able to clearly see what they need to work on and improve. The reason most administrators have a difficult time working with physicians is that they fail to acknowledge the clinical side; data tells the physicians what they need to know. Utilizing it well is a great way to start a conversation.

A second philosophy I swear by is this: a leader must always try to work *on* the company, not *in* the company. Instead of sitting with the units and asking them questions that have nothing to do with you, a better way to spend your time as an executive is to go out and build relationships, connections, and partnerships. Rather than wearing scrubs and involving myself in the day-to-day happenings, I traveled away from the hospital to give lectures and speak at conferences, both nationally and internationally. I acted as the face of the organization, and every time I presented, I talked about my experiences at the Heart Center and what it did better than anyone else in the area. I spoke in Barcelona, Sydney, Stockholm, Vienna, Singapore, Stratford-upon-Avon, and many more places, increasing awareness about the Heart Center and our healthcare models.

When I talk about working *on* the company, this is what I mean; you work to improve the prospects of the company, better situate it in the context of the national and global markets, and bring it the value and recognition it deserves. The hospital employed physician and clinical leaders who were much better suited than I was to lead the everyday operations. By trusting them to do their jobs, I was able to do mine. I put the Heart Center on the radar of most international healthcare organizations, which boosted our referrals, promotional efforts, and partnerships. I frequently reminded myself of this philosophy when anyone gave me grief about not spending enough time down in the units. Everyone knew that my door was always open to come and talk, and I would also frequently make rounds to the different units and process areas. They always knew where to find me.

I may have adopted two leadership principles to guide my own goals, but at the Heart Center, we all operated under one, all-important philosophy: "A patient's *worst* day in the Heart Center should be better than their *best* day at one of our competitors'."

As one of our core missions was to provide the utmost care, I always told our physicians and staff members that if they wanted to continue providing patient-centered care, we first needed to figure out what was right for the patient. Then, if the right course of action seemed like an impossible task, we needed to find a way to make it possible.

Let me tell you of a time when we truly lived this philosophy in service to one of our patients. No matter how efficient a hospital is, there will come a time when not even the best team in the world can save an extremely sick patient. When one such patient passed away in the Heart Center, her husband and daughter were beyond devastated. Grief may be a natural response to loss, but that doesn't make it any easier to witness how hard the daughter struggled to move past the first stage: denial.

I empathized with her pain. Her mother passed away suddenly, and with the daughter living in California, she didn't have a chance to say goodbye. Her denial led her to one conclusion: her mother's death had to be the hospital's fault. She didn't know how or why, but she firmly believed that her mother would have lived if she were not at the Heart Center.

I knew that for her own peace (and for our legal safety), we needed to meet with her and answer all of her questions, no matter how much time it took.

I gathered the key physicians who provided care for her mother, our risk manager, and our director of nursing in one room, and I invited the daughter and her father to attend the meeting and ask us all the questions they had. We sat in that meeting for nearly three hours—that's how much discussion was necessary for the daughter to accept her mother's death. To me, every minute we talked in that room was well spent. Of course, during such an emotional discussion, not one person walked away with dry eyes, but when we tout our quality of care and commitment to patient satisfaction, moments like these validate our mission, vision, and values. It is this dedication to our patients that helped the Heart Center grow into what it is today: a testament to how a healthcare organization can truly turn around its financials and operations to provide the height of care, treatment, and hospitality to those it was built to serve.

Chapter SEVEN
Taking Charge
of Destiny

Toward the end of my six years at the Heart Center of Indiana, it became apparent to both investment groups, the Care Group and St. Vincent, that healthcare as an industry was changing and, naturally, becoming more challenging. As a joint venture, the Heart Center could not participate in St. Vincent's or Ascension's contracts, and without those two behemoths to lean on, maintaining healthy margins morphed into an uphill battle. With this in mind, the two investor groups decided that a change in ownership was the best course.

During this change, Ascension National Health System, the largest nonprofit healthcare system in the country, came into play. Ascension increased its ownership to allow for the organization to negotiate together as opposed to being a competitor.

With the best legal guidance, the transition happened smoothly and in a compliant manner. Since we were now even more accountable to Ascension, Vince Caponi and I sat down together and decided to brand this new entity under a different name. So, I transitioned out of the role of CEO of the Heart Center and into the role of president of what we branded as the St. Vincent Medical Group.

When I entered this new role as president, I remember L. H. Bailey, one of the board chairpersons of the Heart Center, asked me to reflect on how far I had come. I started my career as a registration clerk, worked my way up to serving by the bedside as a respiratory therapist, and I was about to be the president of an organization that housed 1,200 physicians.

I had come a long, long way.

"As CEO of the Heart Center, you had the ability to touch and feel every part of the organization—you could put one hand on one wall and the other hand on another wall, so you were still contained," L. H. Bailey told me. "However, as you move to the St. Vincent Medical Group, you're going to be further removed. You'll no longer be able to touch both sides of the organization with outstretched hands."

It took me less time than I thought to understand what L. H. Bailey was trying to warn me about. At an administrative level, change happens slowly, yet you can lose control very quickly. You need to stay on the edge of your seat constantly, knocking down problems before they can rear their heads.

PEOPLE IN THE RIGHT SEATS

During the merge, tensions ran high—we were merging three huge groups, the Care Group, St. Vincent Physician Network, and CorVasc, into one entity. The physicians and staff in the other groups had already grown reluctant, believing that as the largest of the three groups, the Care Group would be the priority for me and the leadership team, which led to a few tumultuous meetings.

It became clear to me that I had to address this head-on. As often as I could, I told every physician and staff member that no group would be made a "priority." I had to hammer home this point every time I heard a naysayer say anything contrary. It took some time, but with the new mission, vision, and values we developed for the organization, we finally brought team spirit and an inclusive culture to the dynamic.

The common mission, vision, and values we created began to effect change. By incorporating these elements into the workflow and every initiative, we started to establish a cohesive culture of service, quality, and excellence. It brought a fresh energy into the leadership team, and they began to see St. Vincent Medical Group for what it was: something new that was bigger than the individual groups, one of the largest physician-led organizations in the US. The excitement was contagious—shared mission, vision, and values can galvanize an entire organization this way.

I credit the leadership team I inherited for the smooth transition we underwent. Most of the leaders came from the Care Group (so you can see why physicians and staff from the other groups were initially concerned). The CFO and COO of the Care Group, Brian Morris and Brad McNabb, retained their titles as CFO and COO of St. Vincent Medical Group. They assimilated to the new culture of the organization like fish in water. They were skilled, talented, and good at their jobs, and most importantly, they hired the right people for the right teams, a skill that made all the difference.

Speaking of putting people in the right seats, Vince and I had a one-on-one discussion about how to approach the CEO position. As part of the negotiation deal, the Care Group had its own take on who should adopt the role, and while he was an excellent candidate, I told Vince that we couldn't forget an important concept: *form follows function.* Our decision couldn't be a result of historical group size, control, or interpersonal relationships; the only true way to place the right person in the right seat was to consider if they would fit the form of the organization well.

The deciding board had a difficult time choosing one leader from the three heads of each group—the culture of the groups, leadership styles, approaches, and experience were all considered and very much deliberated. Vince was on this team, and I knew he was never one to make a judgment call without looking at it from all angles. He had an executive presence; I never once witnessed him have a knee-jerk reaction to anything. With him on the panel, I knew they would choose the right man. And they did.

In the end, the negotiating team picked Dr. Fogel from the Care Group to be the CEO, and I would step into the role of president.

One of the other two CEOs was the CEO of CorVasc, who actually served as a priest decades prior. Though he left the priesthood ages before, he still carried himself with all the dignity and demeanor of a priest, which brought me to, if I can say so myself, the *excellent* idea of putting him in charge of mission effectiveness. No one has ever fit that position better than he did. In fact, I even had people tell me that he was so perfect in the role, they could almost see him in his Roman collar!

As I evaluated the leadership team, I had the incredible opportunity to work with Lana Lehman, the executive vice president of the Care Group, again. I still remember the first time I met her. I was a senior consultant at Health Evolutions. At the time, Steve Thomas told me, "If you're ever going to do anything in cardiology in Indiana, you need to get to know Lana Lehman."

So, the first thing I did was work with her assistant, Beverly (who would later become my assistant), and admit to her, "My colleagues believe that if I'm to survive, I need to meet Lana." I was even ready to give her a contrite kiss on her ring if it meant I could get on Lana's good side.

Beverly looked at me and said, "I know just the restaurant you can take her to for lunch."

Soon after, Lana and I sat down at Amalfi's, an Italian restaurant, and before we even finished our salads, we were finishing each other's sentences. We shared so much in common: we nursed the same vision for the future of healthcare, and though we were not physicians by background, we both had bedside experience and were responsible for leading physicians. The relationship we developed then remained strong when we both found ourselves working together once again—me, as the new CEO of St. Vincent, and Lana, as the executive vice president of the Care Group and a board member of the Heart Center of Indiana.

Lana was also an incredible mentor, not just to me but to everyone in the organization. She used Stephen Covey's teachings to mentor team members in effectively working towards furthering our mission, vision, and values, as well as easing the challenges they faced in day-to-day operations. She and I also spent considerable time mentoring physician leaders, who were all incredibly brilliant and had well-above-average IQs, but not as excellent EQs. We tag-teamed their mentorships, helping them grow as leaders and develop the interpersonal skills that helped them be more effective and successful. Together, Lana and I made an excellent team, and when she decided that it was time for her to retire and spend time with her grandkids, I made sure to give her the send-off she deserved: a lavish going-away party. The room was packed with not a dry eye in the house. Unsurprisingly, over the years, Lana had positively impacted a lot of people. She was leaving behind a rich career legacy that most of us could only aspire to accomplish.

Dr. Joel Feldman

Chief Medical Director at Managed Health Services Indiana; Former Board Chairman of Acesis; Former Chief of Surgery, CMO, and Regional President at Ascension St. Vincent Hospital Indianapolis; Former Vice Chair of the Department of Surgery at the Heart Center of Indiana

A timeless joke goes around in the healthcare industry: if you ask a surgeon to name the two smartest surgeons in the world, they can never remember the name of the other person. In my experience as a surgeon, I must say that this is, more often than not, the case in most hospitals. Physicians—surgeons, particularly—are so used to being the "captain of the ship" in their own respective specialties, ORs, and clinics that they often assume an authoritative leadership style. Most leaders would've handled the management side by themselves and let the surgeons and physicians stick to treatment—but not John. He believed that physicians can have an impact in every aspect of the organization: quality of care, system growth, and profit margin. In the healthcare industry, medicine may be the product, but that is not what we are selling. Rather, we are in the relationship business, and that is exactly what we sell: relationships.

When John accepted the role of CEO at St. Vincent Heart Center, he immediately jumped in with the thought of a dyad, a collaborative physician-administrative leadership body. The concept was not popular at the time as, back then, medicine had always been considered too important a business to let physicians have significant input. John tirelessly championed this directive, however, and even created programs to teach physicians how to lead, a skill we physicians and surgeons do not pick up during our residencies or education. Not only did John have to make administrative spaces more inclusive of physicians, but he also had to address and mitigate several inefficient ways of problem-solving on the physicians' side. Physicians wanted more successful outcomes, both for patients and team members, but had so many responsibilities and pressures that recognizing these patterns proved difficult. John's coaching addressed both limitations and proficiencies and, through servant leadership, molded accomplished, intelligent physicians into adept leaders as well.

I had the opportunity to attend several of these coaching programs myself. Each lasted for a period of months, and then the next year, John would select a new group. However, I always found myself signed up every year, to which I told John, "I must be a really bad student; you keep sending me back for more coaching!" I wasn't really complaining though—the chance to hear new insights continued to open my eyes about the value and approach needed for a leadership position. On one occasion, we took the TKI assessment and a few other similar tests that categorized us according to certain characteristics—not to box us in, but to give us insight into how we needed to change and in which direction. Without the foundational knowledge gained from these mentorship seminars, I may not have been able to do what I am doing today or learn what I am learning.

John recognized that people are not born leaders, and physicians come from different backgrounds, harbor different personalities, and due to their titles and success, are already ingrained with an authoritative approach to leadership. But he knew this didn't have to be the status quo. Because John always introduces ideas with the rationale behind them and is open to others' ideas while understanding accountability, he earned mutual respect from his physicians, who accepted his viewpoint of having a dyad at the helm. The initiative ultimately brought the St. Vincent Heart Center out of the red and contributed to the further growth and influence of what was already one of the largest and best-known cardiology groups in the country.

On a broader scale, this ambition began a new way of thinking and introduced new questions: How do we make physicians more productive? How can they better contribute to the good of an organization? How do we tap into and expand their skill set?

Anyone who serves in healthcare, even those who are not physicians or healthcare providers, believe that they impact people's lives. Whether they're an accountant, a statistician, or the person who keeps the building lights on, non-clinicians feel strongly that they are contributing to the health and well-being of every single patient. I was rounding on our oncology floor one day and stopped to chat with one of our housekeepers.

When I asked her what she did, she replied, "I prevent infections in cancer patients." Infections can be fatal, so she was right: she was indeed saving lives. This feeling of doing good for society is what drives us all in the work that we do in hospitals, day in and day out—and one look at John's work and leadership style is reflective of this very motive.

The last four years have seen dramatic and accelerating changes in the healthcare delivery system. Costs are skyrocketing, and there is a much greater focus on the bottom line. Physicians have once again been relegated to the clinic, cath lab, and OR where they can generate revenue, excluded from leadership roles. Now, more than ever, we need a John Stewart physician dyad at the helm.

THE TKI ASSESSMENT

I had enormous help from Dr. Dan Lumpkin, PhD, and Dr. Craig Miller, MD, in helping me form the leadership team and developing leadership training for the team at large. After all, leadership and management are responsible for steering the organization, and they needed to be not only the right fit but also well-trained and cognizant of our mission, vision, and values. If they are not crafted intentionally, the entire organization could suffer. So, we ended up using the Thomas-Kilmann Conflict Mode Instrument (TKI) to assess each individual along two dimensions, assertiveness and cooperativeness, and better understand their approaches to conflict resolution.

For example, my TKI profile indicates that I score high in "competing," which is an assertive and power-oriented mode, and lowest in "avoiding," signifying that I'm least likely to avoid or sidestep a conflict. The assessment not only allows individuals to learn more about themselves but also recommends self-reflection questions to think more about what can be improved. I scored medium in the "accommodating" dimension, and the report provided me with a blueprint of what this quality looks like when overused and underused and which questions I need to ask myself to learn more.

You can now see why I recommend and utilize this tool as often as I can. It allows you to understand the different personalities and qualities of the leaders on your team and gives them a resource for self-improvement while allowing you to pair up complementary skill sets together in each project or initiative. Of course, I don't exclusively rely on this tool; more often than not, I use it to validate my instinct. Decades in this career have strengthened my intuition. When we performed the TKI assessment on the leadership team I had assembled and we plotted them on the grid, everyone was surprised to see an even distribution in every dimension! My gut instinct had outdone itself in the selection process and wowed the leaders. Now, they could understand each other better: why some people butted heads more often than others, which approaches appealed to certain members, and how to bring out the best in one another.

LEAD, FOLLOW, OR GET OUT OF THE WAY

I'm sure you're already starting to see how much I was removed from the daily operations of the hospital. Instead, my focus was on the big picture. Of course, I missed being on the frontlines, being immersed in work of service to the team and patients. But as president, I provided an entirely different kind of service—I recognized that I had a much greater pull in directing the organization toward the core values I always insisted on. I had a hand in shaping a culture of mutual trust and respect, driving efforts toward superior quality of care, and enabling physicians and leaders to do what they do best. It was fulfilling work, albeit in a different way.

The bulk of my three years here was spent standardizing definitions, concepts, and processes across the board. Soon, when other leaders carrying out similar work discovered our efforts, Dr. Fogel and I were asked to be a part of a committee for developing a national physician enterprise, one that could take these standardization efforts nationwide. I chaired the Physician Practice Management Subcommittee, and we worked not only for physicians in Indiana but also across the nation. We worked to standardize physician employment agreements, budget reports, statistics, reporting structure, and industry standards—all foundations for a national organization that would soon come into existence.

Every month, we would have an off-site Clinical Leadership Council (CLC) meeting where we collectively discussed the case for building a national physician enterprise. Ultimately, there was a small group of us who became the Practice Management Subcommittee (I served as the chair), but before all that, the real work was being done in the evenings after our CLC meeting. All of us—and this was no small group—

went out for dinner together, got back to the hotel, and then reconvened at the hotel bar. We would talk about everything from culture integration to electronic health records to local markets to physician leadership. It was these monthly post-CLC meetings that eventually catalyzed the formation of a national organization: Ascension Physician Services, which would later morph into Ascension Medical Group.

It was around this time when Ascension hosted a two-day convocation. Since some of us had to arrive a day early for other meetings, I decided to host the attendees that evening at my house for wine tasting and hors d'oeuvres. Nearly 60 to 80 people showed up! Most had congregated in the wine cellar, but I found myself in the kitchen talking with Dr. Ziad Haydar, the chief clinical officer of Ascension Health; Beverly, my assistant; and Evan, an intern. Dr. Haydar informed me that Dr. David Pryor, the chief clinical officer for *all* of Ascension, sent him with an invitation: he wanted to talk to me about taking on a role that would allow me to do the work I was doing at St. Vincent Medical Group on a national level. On hearing where this conversation was heading, Beverly skillfully grabbed Evan by the arm (who was, by this point, on his toes trying to listen in), and led him to the other room, saying, "We don't need to be here for this." I still chuckle when I think about how good of an assistant Beverly was.

It was decided that I would transition to Ascension Physician Services as the senior vice president. But I was adamant about working in a dyad. This was my reasoning: this would be the nation's largest physician enterprise, and I'm not a doctor. How would we build any trust or credibility if we didn't have a physician leader in our ranks? Besides, by having a physician leader in a lateral position to mine, we could have diversity of thought, different areas of accountability and expertise, and better peer-to-peer discussions. Thankfully, they understood where I was coming from, and Dr. Samson Jesudass stepped in as clinical leader. With me as the administrative leader, we formed a unit that brimmed with potential. We shared the same vision, complementary strengths, and mutual trust and respect. Ascension Physician Services emerged from a plan on paper to a real entity with more than 11,000 providers in 24 states!

Unfortunately, we hit a wall almost as soon as we started. During the entire first year, we operated without a budget and very few resources. If we needed to fulfill certain operating costs, Dr. Pryor, the CEO, or the CFO of the Ascension Health System had to approve it. But they were busy people with busy schedules, and the delays were nerve-wracking. The bureaucracy stifled progress, and there seemed to be no workaround. As someone who has always been a "do it" person and not a "wait for someone else to do it" kind of person, I felt incredibly frustrated without control over my own actions and decisions. I've always been a believer in the sentiment of the saying: "Lead, follow, or get out of the way." But in such a place, I couldn't do any of the three. My hands were tied. All I could do was barely avoid the landmines and try to stay afloat in the whirlpool of politics.

Certain challenges, especially when you're trying to get a hold of competing entities within the organization, grow to astronomical levels when you're leading a national-level corporation. The aforementioned politics of upper-level management is an absolute beast to contend with. I began to notice the inherent friction of the people—half the organization didn't want me there because they believed I was there to take their jobs or make their lives more difficult. I had worked in enough organizations (and in my backyard at the old Kentucky house) to know when the roots were rotten.

When I entered Ascension, the established leadership only had eyes for power and control, not service. This completely went against my personal values. As you know, if there's one thing I never did, it was exert control over doctors or team members. Yet, in this organization, it seemed like control was the modus operandi.

While most of the time it felt like I had no say in my own decision-making, I did fight tooth and nail for certain initiatives because I could see the potential for large-scale impact. One of them included launching our promising project, Athena, an electronic health record that was rolled out to all the providers across Ascension's entire system. Nothing of that scale had ever been done before and never so quickly. We completed the Athena project 18 months ahead of schedule, saved millions in expense reductions, and gained millions in revenue enhancement. Even years after I stepped down, Ascension is still Athena's largest client. I mean, how could it not be when it completely revolutionized the way we aggregated and saw operational details right down to the individual provider? I could pull up any provider halfway across the country and tell you exactly what their performance metrics looked like, all while sitting in my office in St. Louis!

I was serving as an interim COO for Health Management Associates Physician Group, an organization in Florida with about 1,600 physicians in 18 states, when the leadership at Athenahealth approached me. They requested that I transition to Ascension to implement Athena across the nation. To put it lightly, the opportunity felt like a massive leap in my career. I mean, there are large organizations, and then there are *Ascension-on-steroids* large. It was then that I met John Stewart, my direct supervisor, and Dr. David Pryor, *his* supervisor.

At first, the Athenahealth project saw a bit of pushback from local markets, which took a long time to buy in as we were taking away their "toys" and folding them into an unfamiliar structure. To counter this, we boosted physician engagement: the doctors were the decision-makers, and the administrative team was the facilitator.

For this same reason, all of us under Dr. Pryor had to have a physician partner. My partner, a pediatric rheumatologist, and I would co-lead all of the affinity groups around clinical content with the aim of doctor-to-doctor communication. I covered the administrative side while my partner worked with doctors, which was an effective way of attaining physician buy-in while promoting consistency and transparency. I could help with the configuration of systems, but if a doctor struggled to adopt the technology properly, my partner could coach them through how to use it in a way they found understandable.

Despite the effectiveness of this system, Ascension, being so large, was still a complex matrix. Every decision had to go through multiple filters. Is it compliant? Is it ethical? Is it clinically relevant? Will it increase the doctor's workflow? Is it the right thing to do for the patient? Thankfully, dividing the organization into the clinical side and the administrative side helped push through those filters since both clinical and administrative viewpoints were considered at every level.

As a leader, John saw himself as the remover of these barriers, which isn't the norm in most large organizations. In our monthly accountability meetings, he could have very well adopted the attitude of, "Hey, you're three days late on this project. When will it be done?"

Instead, he always asked, "What do you need from me?"

Transparency was valued above all else. I quickly learned that if something was going to blow up, all I needed to do was inform John. He'd try to understand the situation and then simply ask, "What are we going to do to take care of it?"

While overseeing the implementation of such a huge undertaking as Athena, driving patient care became my number-one reason for getting up in the mornings. And John only enabled that mission. On several occasions, he empowered me to lead massively impactful initiatives, one of which included increasing breast cancer screenings by 20 percent across the nation using Athena. Due to that effort, we found more than 700 women with stage 2 breast cancer who most likely would not have been diagnosed as the lumps in their breasts were not big enough to be noticeable. This is just one instance of many where I felt like my team and I drove remarkable change.

John's service as a leader can be summarized in one story. To provide some context, you need to understand that each of the Ascension ministries had their own unique feel. Austin, for example, was incredibly liberal. In contrast, Detroit was more traditional, and a month from going live in the Detroit market, we still weren't getting the level of cooperation we needed. I'll never forget being in a conference room one day when John picked up the phone and called the Ascension leaders, hospital leaders, and practice leaders. He forced the discussion to take place: "Alright, this is what the issue is. Let's address any comments." In a quick, concise way, he reset the project in that market. Once again, he opened communication lines that were blocked by a desire for bureaucratic control, in part due to the many relationships he'd cultivated throughout his career.

Physician leadership coursed through each of our efforts, and that's in no small part to John's principles. When you can engage physicians around what they've been *trained* to do and what they *want* to do, all while removing administrative bureaucracy, they stop feeling like their practice is a job. After all, no one wants their doctor to be a factory worker, right? Physicians who focus on the quality of care, rather than the number of visits they do in a day, center their work around patient outcomes. And they also become far, far happier.

Despite the success of the Ascension Medical Group, some people never bought into it. These were the executives with one-track minds: no amount of discussions or data would convince them that the organization was a good thing, not a system designed to take away their power.

To put it bluntly, I felt miserable in my role at Ascension, despite some of the incredible people I worked with and the potential I saw for the organization. Due to the suffocating political structure, no leader could enact any kind of change without abusing their positional authority. The culture did not prioritize mutual trust and respect, unlike past organizations I had dedicated myself to before. So, when I realized that I could not facilitate large-scale change in a productive way, that I had little autonomy, and that I could not directly impact the quality of patient care, I knew it was time to leave. I'm not a quitter, but I recognize the necessity of leaving a job or a situation where you cannot add value, gain happiness, or work toward your personal mission and values. There's no point in staying stagnant and wringing your hands helplessly. I knew there were other roles where I could make a difference and bring value, so I took control of my destiny. And it was the best decision I could have made.

Charlie Munger, vice chairman of Berkshire Hathaway and Warren Buffett's closest business partner, died on November 28, 2023, at the age of 99. In some of his final writings, he advised, "You particularly want to avoid working directly under somebody you don't admire and don't want to be like . . . Generally, your outcome in life will be more satisfactory if you work under people whom you correctly admire."[5]

This is why it's so important to know your strengths and weaknesses. Being aware of yourself, what you want, where you fit in, and how you function is important to empower yourself and make decisions that influence not only your life but the lives of others. So many stay entrenched in a bad situation or job, no matter how many times they butt heads against a wall. I had spent 34 loyal years with the Daughters of Charity and Ascension organizations, but when I saw where they were headed, cutting ties didn't seem optional—I knew that I could do no more there. I recalled what my father used to tell me: "Son, to me, you're taller than the trees." If I could be taller than the trees, I could stay steadfast to my values, and I could remain strong and unwavering in my mission.

Every action they took opposed my personal values. And over the years, I've found that when there's no alignment, someone's got to go. This time, that someone was me. I closed a long, long chapter of my life.

At the same time, I also took root and started a new one.

Chapter EIGHT
Taller than the Trees

I have always been a big advocate of leveraging technology in pursuit of high-quality patient care with effective leadership. I'm excited by the potential of new tech and data tools that can allow hospitals to quantify and codify operations, satisfaction, and various other elements such as financials, clinical data, and everything in between. Whenever possible, I've tried my utmost to contribute toward the implementation of such tools and databases in nearly every one of my leadership positions.

It's a *need*—the impact of which I saw directly: physicians and nurses found the data illuminating; patients could share their experience through honest feedback and ratings; and leadership found these tools provided an incredible bird's-eye view of the organization. Tech is often underestimated by hospitals, many hesitating to add yet another expense line item, but I passionately advocate for how such tools continually, time and again, outweigh the cost.

When I left Ascension, I had the opportunity to more thoroughly participate in bringing such healthcare technology to the forefront. Three incredible health tech companies—Privis Health, Acesis, and PolicyStat—all asked me to sit on their boards. (All at different points in my career and "retirement.") By now, I'm sure you know how the opportunity to effect positive change attracts me like a moth to a flame. I couldn't say no. And even if I could, I definitely wouldn't have. An opportunity to improve the quality and transparency of patient care? That's the name of the game for me. It is my personal driving force, my internal mission, vision, and values. And I'm so glad I served on these various boards because these were a few of the most gratifying roles I had ever taken on during my career.

While I couldn't legally sit on the boards of Acesis and PolicyStat during my tenure at Ascension due to the inherent conflict of interest, I was able to officially take my place on their boards once I left my previous role. Before then, I had the opportunity to coach and mentor at several organizations for about 20 years.

But here's where the sequence of events gets a little blurry. Serving on the boards of Privis, Acesis, and PolicyStat; starting my consulting business, t4; and eventually launching and ending Arete Provider Network all overlapped in time. I consulted for Privis for about four years before taking a seat on its boards, and during that time, I simultaneously juggled multiple balls. And for the most part, I served on these boards while I was, technically, in "retirement." (In quotes because, if you saw me then and how busy I was, I doubt anyone would know I was retired.)

This time of my life was a web of different roles, organizations, and responsibilities, and each experience gave me better insight and outlook into how organizations and their leaders tick—and what changes need to be made to guide them down the path of achieving their mission, vision, and values.

All this to say: don't break your head trying to figure out the timeline of these events. (I'll try to give you a loose timeline, but it's not all cut and dry. So, bear with me.) To me, the most important part of these events was the knowledge and insights gained and the relationships I developed. Let me begin with the several boards I served on.

FROM ADMINISTRATION TO INNOVATION

Through my various positions as a board member at different organizations, not only was I able to channel my passion for helping others, but I also utilized my strengths as a strategic thinker. I found ways to hardwire quality into organizations and instill cultures of safety and transparency with the help of my teams, even with all the complexity and confidentiality structures of healthcare industries—in essence, not easy work but extremely edifying.

One of our cardiologists in Indianapolis and the first CEO of Acupera, later to be known as Privis Health, had set up Privis's services as an electronic way of managing clinical pathways and creating a data repository that could be used to define and trigger suggestions for strategies based on best practices. As I said before, it was industry-defining work that perfectly aligned with my own passions. So, when he requested my consulting services, I, of course, said yes and continued to mentor and consult with them even long after there was a change in leadership.

I also sat on the boards of a tech startup company, PolicyStat. It was incredible to see how much this organization grew and achieved before being acquired. I mean, I saw PolicyStat *before* it was PolicyStat, and even then, I knew that the leadership team was onto something remarkable. In fact, the Heart Center of Indiana served as a development laboratory for PolicyStat and was one of their early clients! Guiding the executives at PolicyStat to see the value they're bringing and helping them put their vision into action was the reason I got out of bed every day—not to mention, it gave me the opportunity to actively work on my passions.

It was around this time that I was also introduced to Acesis, and similarly, I saw the flexibility in technology it brought in right away. I wasn't the only one who saw the potential either; my chief medical officer at the Heart Center, Bill Storer, also agreed that this tool could help codify quality management and lead peer review efforts. The action forward was clear—we would partner up with them. However, because of this partnership, my sitting on its board would be a conflict of interest. As soon as I parted ways with Ascension, it freed me up to serve on the board. I continue to serve the organization now, even in retirement. Even during those partnership days, as a client, I still found a way to coach and mentor the organization. I couldn't help it—both Acesis and PolicyStat were creating pioneering new technology that was filling a critical, niche need in quality management, improvement, and safety. If there was any work being done in scaling quality, I had to be there.

Working on these tech startup boards, especially when I had felt stifled by the bureaucracy and slow progress in large organizations, felt truly freeing, inspiring, and purpose-driven. That's not to say everything was smooth sailing. During my experience with consulting and being a board member, I witnessed first-hand some of the big mistakes organizations tend to make with their boards. The most prominent two? *Size and bureaucracy*.

Some hospitals were notorious for having 20-member boards; once a board expands beyond about five people, it becomes unmanageable. Sometimes, they fail to realize that just like any leadership team, a board consists of individuals who all have their own strengths, weaknesses, desires, and missions.

To give you an idea of the diversity present, I have seen people from all industries take board positions. Board members didn't only consist of people from the healthcare industry but rather were chosen based on their specific skill sets and who could best contribute to an organization's various subcommittees. However, if they weren't vetted thoroughly enough or chosen with care, then the numbers added up, and suddenly, the organization would find an entire village sitting in the boardroom. Such big boards slow things down, and besides, it's nearly impossible to freely share ideas, have conversations, or even reach a consensus on action items. When there are no relationships of mutual trust and respect, forget cooperation and teamwork; power and control end up being the main operating procedures.

In such cases, developing understanding is necessary. I often used those tools I discussed in earlier chapters—the TKI, particularly—to help people understand who they are and who their fellow members are. Additionally, these tools also came in handy when we needed to assess the composition of the board and make them aware of how they fit into the culture and how they could best support its success.

NORTH STAR

While I've coached and mentored hundreds of people—physicians, executives, staff, and board members alike—I've also been the recipient. I do for them what my mentors did for me, mentors like Kathy Rowan, Sister Irene Kraus, Lana Lehman, and Vince Caponi, to name a few. My main motivation to help people arises from them. I want to pay their kindness, generosity, patience, and wisdom forward and support the mission, vision, and values of people, just as they enriched my goals.

This same trickle-down effect of mentorship was embedded in the very structure of my consulting company, t4. I started t4 primarily because of my consultancy work. I realized that rather than having my salary come in through my social security, a pass-through LLC would work more conveniently. That way, if I needed to hire freelancers or contractors, I could do so through one umbrella entity. I formed t4 before I left Ascension, knowing that pretty soon, I was either going to leave, retire, or both.

At that point, I was 63, which, to me, is too early to retire—my father had instilled in me that it's when you don't stay engaged with something that you die.

I had seen some of my friends transition into retirement, and while some handled it better than others, I could see how much it changed them. I had no desire to sit in front of a TV all day and not leave my couch. So, no, I didn't plan to stop working anytime soon. I still craved the opportunity to work with high-impact organizations that were making innovative strides in healthcare. Consulting and coaching felt like the right avenue.

When I tell people about t4, their first question is always: "Why did you call it t4?" This just so happens to be my favorite question because it gives me an excuse to talk about my father.

My dad often said, "Son, to me, you've grown taller than the trees." That's where the name of my consulting company, t4, comes from: *Taller Than The Trees*. We designed the logo with this in mind as well. My niece helped me choose the Japanese lettering that means "tall trees" to represent the brand, and she also brought the company's website to life.

Through t4, I was able to codify what I had been doing for years with more intention and devote myself wholly to the task.

One of my core philosophies when coaching is to simply listen. The best coaches listen more than they talk, and when that happens, it turns into a conversation rather than a one-sided lesson, which may not even be what the client is looking for. You'd be surprised how much simple conversations help; I've even had people on some of my flights ask me to coach them simply because I listened to their challenges at length. And some of these instances were closer to home too.

My landscaper, who owns and runs his own business, was working in my yard one day when we struck up a friendly conversation, just shooting the bull. After talking for a bit, he asked, "Would you mind if I came over for a cup of coffee one day to pick your brain?" When he arrived, we were just meeting as friends—there was no coaching service set up. He told me about the challenges of running his business and his plans for the future, and just by listening, it somehow developed into a coaching relationship!

Listening is a skill I try to instill in all of my clients. When there's friction, senior executives are often of the mindset that they need to be doing all of the talking. That's not the case. Truly effective leaders understand that they need to listen and ask more questions. And those questions can help de-escalate the tension and arrive at the root of the problem.

One of the main issues executives come to me for is to understand and get a better handle on turnover. Whenever that happens, my first move is to make it clear to them that people leave a job not because of money but because of their manager. There are three reasons why people accept leadership positions: control, mission, or money. To be clear, none of these reasons are right or wrong. But depending on the combination of motives, the leader either attracts and retains talent or drives it away. The type of leaders notorious for this are controllers—if you noticed, I quickly left organizations when a controller was in charge. Controllers are, more often than not, responsible for turnover. So, if an executive comes to me with this issue, I work with them to ease out of the pattern of micromanaging—they need to be working *on* the company, not *in* the company.

CEOs tend to struggle when unsure of how to identify the root of an issue. That's why my go-to advice is to encourage them to ask questions before taking action. Often, when they *understand* what they want, they can *enact* it within the organization, either by operating within an established structure or finding a novel way of making it work. Understanding an issue, problem, or roadblock—whatever it may be—is paramount.

To rid themselves of controlling behaviors, however, they must first gain awareness. Once again, the TKI tool comes in handy. A portion in the back of the assessment recommends an individualized work plan that takes into account their strengths, weaknesses, and available growth opportunities to help fulfill the team's needs. These personal corrective action plans would suggest a controlling individual start developing the habit of not only recognizing their traits but also using them to create situations where they are *participating* and not micromanaging. As a coach, I talk leaders through these plans and help them establish month-by-month goals, and we meet often to work through whatever challenges arise when they begin to enact the much-needed change.

Of course, every client I coach gets a spiel on the leadership quality that is very near and dear to my heart: any decision a leader makes should be rooted in the company's mission, vision, and values. There has to be a guiding North Star, so the leaders know which direction they need to strive for. I tell them, "Once you have your North Star, it's about developing culture. Your mission, vision, and values will attract the right talents for your organization." At a board or executive level, the job then becomes teaching, mentoring, and getting out of their way.

ARETE PROVIDER NETWORK

As I coached through t4, talking to and mentoring executives proved something to me: the mission, vision, and values we had developed at Ascension Medical Group were in the right ballpark. There was something remarkable there; I was sure of it.

The healthcare professionals and physicians I spoke with agreed with me heartily. The healthcare industry needed a quality-focused organization. Badly. So, I decided to pull together a catalyst event at Passalacqua Winery in California and booked a boardroom for a day-long meeting. (Of course, a wine tasting was included.)

I brought together a group of executives, notably among them were Brian Morton, Jason Haugen, and other team members. I told them all about how we could put together a structure that improved healthcare and quality and lowered costs at the same time. It was a need—that was indisputable. While this mission had once failed to materialize, who was to say it couldn't happen at all? Why not start an organization dedicated to this goal?

It was from this conversation that the Arete Provider Network was born.

When I left Ascension, I felt frustrated and disappointed that I couldn't make the impact I had hoped. The driving force in starting Arete was to essentially drive major impacts. And the main mission I hoped to energize? *Physician leadership.* I firmly believed then, and continue to believe now, that with physicians at the helm, organizations could achieve high quality at a low cost, all while maintaining phenomenal safety data points and experience. To put it simply, physician leaders should be equipped to always do what's right for the patient. I had witnessed this for myself at the Heart Center. Politics had no say, insurance had no say, and no one dictated what needed to be done for the patient except for the physicians who knew best. I don't like it when bureaucracy and politics get in the middle of a patient-doctor relationship. That relationship is what embodies the sanctity of healthcare.

With that vision, we launched Arete and found a lot of support for what we wanted to do from other healthcare organizations and physicians alike. We even started working with multiple groups to form partnerships with or even acquire them.

Only, while we set that up . . . the world turned upside down. The COVID-19 pandemic was upon us. Before we knew it, investors started pulling out, and we had no choice but to shutter the organization.

And then, at the same time, I received a call from my sister-in-law.

That changed everything.

Chapter NINE
Eight Surgeries in Eight Months

My older brother, Bob, was the biggest Iditarod fan. It all started when he went on an Alaskan cruise with his wife, Susan. In one of the stops on the cruise, they attended a talk by Lance Mackey, a musher who had won the Iditarod races *four* times. Mackey told his audience how mushing and taking care of dogs saved his life from drug abuse. His motivational speech brought tears to everyone's eyes, and by the end of the talk, Bob was absolutely enamored with the man and the sport that meant so much to him. He bought all his books and CDs and started watching the races religiously. For his 70th birthday, when he, Susan, and I shared a hot air balloon ride, we presented him with a gift: a card that included two tickets to the ceremonial dog race. Bob was *ecstatic*.

The ceremonial dog race was on a Saturday. We attended the event too and lined up with all the other mushers—Bob all the way up in the front and me somewhere in the middle. As I waited to get in my sled, I turned around and saw Bob's favorite musher, Lance Mackey! He was not mushing in the race, however, due to his illness, but I did get the chance to take a picture with him.

From that moment on, Bob never stopped talking about our Alaska trip, a time when he was so healthy and full of life. However, his health had been deteriorating for a while due to an early life-changing experience. Being nine years older than me, he had joined the Air Force and was shipped out to the Da Nang Air Base in Vietnam when I was in the fifth grade. There, he had significant exposure to Agent Orange—in his words, they'd "spray the perimeter with it" and "soak the soldiers' fatigues," which they'd then wear all day long in the hot, humid weather. Much later in life, my brother was diagnosed with several illnesses as a result, colon cancer only being one of them. With how close Bob and I were, you can imagine how quickly I dropped everything to go to him when I heard the news from Susan that he was taken to the ER.

On the phone, Susan told me they found a tumor the size of a grapefruit, and I knew there wasn't much time left. I focused all my energy on selling my house in Naples and moving in with my brother to be his caregiver. Susan owned her own accounting firm, and it was tax season—there was simply no way she could juggle these two big responsibilities all by herself.

I dedicated myself to looking after them for three months, not doing much of anything else in the meantime—work or otherwise. After he passed, I stayed with Susan for a month longer, supporting her during this time of mourning. But I knew Bob well; he had lived his entire life by a strong faith system and accepted death with grace. I decided to move on too, but the question was . . . where? And what next?

When people ask me why I decided to move to Charleston, my honest, straight-from-the-heart answer is, "I don't know." It just seemed to happen. I had never stepped foot in Charleston before I moved, but I knew the city met some important criteria: it was close to the ocean, the temperature rarely dropped below freezing, and it had a great food scene. Not to mention, while I was living with Bob and Susan, I became a lot closer to Susan's family who mostly all lived in South Carolina.

We went through a difficult time together when Bob passed, and since I was the last one standing in my family, they simply said, "We'll just adopt you into ours." Moving to Charleston meant that though I lost a sibling, I could still be close to the people I cared about. Every piece of the puzzle seemed to fit just right, and even though I'd never seen the city for myself, I had a good feeling about it.

When I met my realtor (who, coincidentally, was also from Bowling Green, Kentucky), I told him I wanted a house that had character. So far, all the houses I had lived in were newly constructed, which made me feel like I was living inside a model house catalog. I wanted a *home* this time. One that had a few dings and that I could furnish to be less like an *Architectural Digest* exhibit and more like a comfortable place to rest and stay warm. You know—how a home is actually supposed to be. He found me the perfect place: a World War II bungalow built in 1945. Hearing that it was in a great neighborhood where everybody knew everybody, I bought the house without even walking through it first. I based my decision entirely on pictures online, and I don't regret a thing.

To this day, I firmly believe that the universe brought me to Charleston for two reasons: the Medical University of South Carolina, also known as MUSC, and the most wonderful neighbors I gained through the move.

THE WAITING

One month after moving in, I woke up to unbearable abdominal pain in the middle of the night. Thinking an old hiatal hernia had flared up again, I took some antacids and returned to bed. Except the pain didn't subside—it only became worse and worse until it grew into a sharp, burning agony unlike anything I'd ever experienced. I called 911, and before long, EMTs wheeled me into one of the four ambulances that flashed its lights in front of my house. In the ER, doctors diagnosed me with stage 3 cirrhosis.

My liver was functioning at 10 percent.

I needed a liver transplant.

And if I didn't get one in time, I would have three months to live.

The process of getting a liver transplant, however, is one of the most cumbersome systems to exist. It's incredibly daunting for the patient. Imagine being in pain and fatigued and yet needing to get tests done again and again simply to *qualify* for a transplant. After that, there are more meetings and doctor's appointments to attend and then, finally, the *waiting*, which drags on for months. Overall, the process to get listed and then receive a transplant can take up to 11 months, by which point, if a patient's condition is bad enough, they would have already passed away, as many unfortunately do while hoping to receive that life-saving phone call where the person on the other end says, "We found one for you."

I, however, could not wait that long. The words "three months to live" hung over my head, meaning my life depended on me taking matters into my own hands to compress the process as much as possible. When I first heard my diagnosis, I felt like I had been hit upside the head—I never drank much, so I couldn't believe I had cirrhosis.

I expressed my disbelief to Dr. Koch, my transplant physician, to which he replied, "John, why does it matter *how* you got it? You just need to move forward with your life." I decided to take his advice—there is a stigma around alcoholism and liver transplants where patients can get stuck in a loop of trying to rationalize their diagnosis. I couldn't let that be me, especially when I needed to take care of myself.

So, despite how tired I felt, I made sure to schedule tests and appointments back-to-back. I'm talking about as many as 11 appointments a day. Sometimes, when Susan would accompany me to get these tests done, she would say, "John, let me get your wheelchair." As stubborn as I am, I kept insisting on walking so I could keep my strength up. More than once, she said I wasn't "looking good," but I didn't take it too personally—if anything, that just made me want to walk even more!

To get listed for a transplant, I had to go through a full workup—CT and MRI scans, upper and lower endoscopies, checks for cancer cells, and so on—so the results could be used to generate a MELD score. This MELD score was then used to determine my transplant eligibility.

To be considered "eligible," a patient needs a MELD score of 14.

My score was 29, though it lowered to 23 around the time I got listed.

If I didn't receive a transplant soon, I wasn't going to make it. However, one of the coordinators informed me they had patients with MELD scores as high as 30 still waiting to be put up for a transplant.

A MELD score of 30? I thought. *I'm already so sick—I can't wait that long.* I had to talk to my physician.

"Why would you wait until I've got one foot in the grave?" I asked Dr. Koch. "I've been in this career long enough to know that the higher the MELD score, the higher the mortality and morbidity rates. Would I not recover faster if you did it sooner, while I'm still strong enough to survive it and heal quicker?"

"John, you're right," Dr. Koch said. He decided to vouch for me and took up the case with the committee. I felt somewhat relieved, knowing that I have always been my best advocate. But the entire time, I could only think about patients who hadn't worked in healthcare for as long as I had. What about those who aren't informed well enough? How do they advocate for themselves?

Thankfully, since my physician personally believed I was a great candidate and the psychologists I had to meet with as a part of the process could attest to the fact I was a "minimal risk" for relapsing or drinking again, they were able to expedite my waiting time. My MELD score was then presented to a transplant committee, which, as a whole, decided whether or not I could be approved to be listed. I had to spend hours discussing with the committee, and they questioned me about everything from my health records to my lifestyle to my support network.

Finally, after much deliberation, I received word that I was approved and officially listed to get a transplant. Now all I had to do was to keep my phone close to me, rest, and wait to hear when a donor was available. So sick that I only had the energy to move from either the couch to my bed or vice versa, I kept my phone close by.

Even the opportunity to rest was taken from me, though, when yet another health issue cropped up: my right eye was starting to go blind. When I went to the ER at the local hospital, they informed me that I could possibly have a retinal tear, but they didn't have the capacity to perform the necessary surgery. So, where did I end up? Right back at the MUSC emergency room. I needed immediate surgery, or I would lose my eyesight. And during all this, I was on so many medications that they first had to do multiple tests to prepare me for anesthesia and surgery. They even had to do my eye surgery in the main OR of the hospital just in case of any complications—that way, the ICU would be just a floor away. My stress levels at this point were, obviously, at an all-time high. I was waiting to hear back regarding my transplant, and now the possibility of me going blind in one eye was very real.

While I found a way to somehow cope with it all, I did sometimes feel like there was no way I could make it through all this. During those times, one of my lifelong friends would always offer to come and look after me—he was retired and living alone and wanted to help me recover after my surgeries. I'm so thankful for such friends who acted as an unshakeable support system for me. Most of all, it was them who gave me the strength to persist.

FOUR DAYS

Three months after being listed and after my right eye surgery, I heard back from the transplant committee. I still remember that call. At about 9:30 one morning, my phone rang and the caller ID showed an 843 area code. I knew exactly who that was.

"John, we think we have a match," said the person on the other end of the line. It was the hospital. They went through a list of lab values and other metrics to make it clear to me that they found a compatible match. Typically, they would also let the patient know if there were any known illnesses, and fortunately, there were none in my case. I was lucky that I had such a donor. They waited for me to approve it based on all the criteria. The entire time, I was on edge, and equal parts stress and optimism built up inside of me. Once I approved it, they asked, "How soon can you get here?"

As soon as I heard that, my feelings reached a crescendo: relief, excitement, anxiety, fear. But I had no time to dwell on any of that. I needed to go. Thankfully, we had a plan for this very situation. I immediately dialed the number of my neighbor, whom I had promised I would call so she could take me to the hospital. Then, we called up my friend in Louisville who already had a bag packed up and ready to go, and my next-door neighbor came over to look after Bently until my friend could get to the house. Everyone moved so quickly and settled into their roles so efficiently that it felt like a complex army operation. But they all pulled it off.

At the hospital, doctors prepped me for the transplant. And by "prep," I mean they completely knocked me out. For *four days*. So far, none of this had been easy. So, of course, neither was this procedure. It was only when I woke up, all groggy and exhausted, that I found out there had been major complications with the operation: right after the surgery, my blood pressure dropped dramatically, and I was bleeding out internally. When I was taken back into the OR, they removed a blood clot the size of a grapefruit. Clearly, grapefruit is not my fruit. My brother had a tumor the size of a grapefruit, I had a clot the size of a grapefruit, and I can't even eat them anymore after my surgery!

Jokes aside, the situation had become quite dire. The doctors were so worried that they even started preparing my friends and family for the possibility of me not making it. I had a will prepared and made sure my affairs were in order. As a Catholic, I was even given my last rites. No career in healthcare or otherwise could have prepared me for the horrified feeling I experienced as I heard all of this after the fact, still coming down from the morphine and medications.

Even before learning about this, the situation put me through tremendous mental trauma. The drugs messed with my mind so deeply that when I finally came off them, I asked, confused, "Did I not have my surgery?" That's how much they had addled my brain.

During those four days, I also experienced dark and disturbing hallucinations—dreams so vivid and detailed that I genuinely believed them to be real. Once I was off the respirator, I was able to tell my friends about my visions. One hallucination had me convinced that my caregivers were trying to kill me. Another made me believe that I was "watching TV" by staring into a corner of my room . . . only to have someone tell me that there was no TV there.

"It's all in your head, John," they told me.

I was so disoriented that I couldn't even tell what was real anymore.

I spent nine days in the hospital, steadily working toward recovery. I was getting better, but there was no breath of relief yet—this time, my *left* eye was failing. Once again, I needed surgery immediately. Even before I could begin to recover from *that* surgery, I soon had *another* minor setback: I developed chronic kidney disease. Stage 3 kidney failure. And I knew there was no way my mind or body could endure another organ transplant. I was running low on strength. But again, I tried to keep a positive outlook. After all, the physicians and nurses always commended me on my ability to stay positive, even while enduring so much pain and suffering. I wasn't going to stop now. I was admitted into MUSC once again for observation while the physicians tried to find a solution.

However, this particular upset confused me. I had never had any kidney problems before. When I informed the doctors, they soon narrowed down the cause: it was one of the many anti-rejection drugs they put me on post-transplant. This drug attacked my kidneys. Within just a couple of days of putting me on a different drug, my kidneys were returning to normal function. Finally, *finally*, my body began to recover.

Even now, months after my surgeries, I can't help but get a little emotional at the challenges I had to go through. During my expansive career in healthcare, I not only saw transplants but also started transplant programs. It was this experience that made me truly appreciate the quality of care I received at MUSC. That's not to say it didn't have its fair share of issues: their ER was always packed to the brim. *Always*. But still, their patient care and values were commendable.

I experienced a perfect example of leadership culture at MUSC. One night when my surgeon was on his shift, he came in to check on me. I had just used the bedside commode. Imagine my utter disbelief when he walked right in and, with all sincerity, offered to help clean me up!

I said to him, laughing, "It's every hospital CEO's dream to have his surgeon wipe his ass!" I mean, talk about a patient-first approach. Everyone from the interns to the clinicians to the CEO at MUSC carried this value in their work, from the time they walked through the hospital doors to the time they finished their tireless shifts. And it showed.

A few months after my last surgery, for the first time in what felt like forever, I didn't have to go to the hospital in panic. I went in for my check-in exams, and with every visit, I saw improvement. This dark time in my life was thankfully coming to a close.

These eight months were hell. But as my body grew stronger and they started to wean me off some of my drugs, I was much, much healthier.

I had a new lease on life. And I was going to spend it doing what I loved: traveling. Eating great food. Taking afternoon naps. And spending time with those I love—family, friends, and Bently.

AFTERWORD

So far, my life has been long and full of ups and downs, challenges and accomplishments, happiness and solemnity. Now, in retirement, I feel so . . . good. Mentally, physically, spiritually, and emotionally. And I want to continue doing good, in my own way, for myself and others. It was in the midst of these feelings that I decided to write a book and share my stories.

Looking ahead, I don't necessarily have a set plan. In fact, it's the opposite; I'm completely open and welcoming of whatever the future may bring. A close friend, also facing retirement, and I were talking about the next phase of our life journeys. He gave me this profound quote by Joseph Campbell, which fit perfectly:

"We must let go of the life we have planned, so as to accept the one that is waiting for us."[6]

I've referred to it often as I start to realize that I no longer live according to someone else's time. Maybe that is why so many people I know who retire focus a whole lot more on grandchildren. I feel strongly that as we age, we owe it to others to pass on our lessons learned and give back, given all we have received.

A few days before writing this afterword, I watched the 2023 CNN Heroes broadcast, an incredible award ceremony that commemorates ordinary people who make extraordinary contributions to the world. One of these stories covered the winner of the ceremony, Dr. Kwane Stewart. Dr. Stewart is a veterinarian who set up a process where he would regularly go out to the street and take care of pets for the homeless. You've read about Bently enough times in this book to know my complete adoration for dogs.

From the very beginning, the segment struck a chord with me. Dr. Stewart was caring for a homeless man's dog when, in the middle of their conversation, the man admitted he hadn't eaten in two days. Dr. Stewart said that since he was going out to lunch soon anyway, he could buy a meal for them both. True to his word, he soon returned with two sandwiches—one for himself and the other for the homeless man. Despite being hungry, the homeless man took out the sandwich from the container, tore off a small corner piece for himself, and handed the rest of the sandwich to his dog. The capacity to empathize that humans have within them is simply astounding. No matter how little one might have, there's always something to give.

Throughout my career, it is this mentality of giving and serving that has kept me on the straight and narrow. Even when I had to leave certain roles, I saw it as a positive. I could find a new place that really needed me, and I could serve yet another group of people and uplift them. And I hope that after reading my story, it gives you the strength to pursue the calling of service as well.

As you give back, I also want to encourage you to take some time to relax and escape from the noise. Soak in the universe. Lately, the weather here in Charleston has been incredible. Some afternoons, I sit on my sun porch, lean back in my recliner, listen to the gentle sounds of running water nearby, and drift off into the most satisfying naps. Retirement is treating me well, clearly.

After being told by multiple people over the years that I should write a book from my experiences, I thought to myself, *Why not now, in retirement?* But I'm not exactly one to sit down at a computer and "bang out" a book. Working with Ed Trifone, Arya Dixit, and Jamie Fleming at BrightRay Publishing taught me to enjoy the process. Their unique approach is to "pull the book out of your head." I was finally able to lay bare all my stories and insights.

And now that *Taller than the Trees* is a reality . . . maybe I'll try fiction?

SUPPLY AND DEMAND:
An Official Ask for Organ Donation

I am embarrassed to admit, especially given my long career in healthcare, that there was once a time when I never checked the organ donation box on my driver's license. I can't believe how selfish that was, considering that I am only here, healthy and well, because someone else had selflessly checked that same box.

In the United States, 103,327 people are on the national transplant waiting list. One donor can save 8 lives and enhance 75 more.[7] That's making a big, big difference. It's a service of the highest kind. In a matter of life and death, you are making way for life . . . all by saying yes at the DMV when they ask you if you would like to donate your organs in the case of a fatality.

I want to encourage you, reader, as someone who has experienced my story through this book, to consider registering as an organ donor. I now have it stated clearly in my living will, but that's not necessary—checking a simple box is all it takes.

I am eternally grateful for my donor as they made this book, my life, and my happiness possible. I can only repay them by paying it forward. And when the time comes, I hope I can help someone else the same way.

A small yes can save many lives. I am living proof.

Follow this link for more information, resources, and support regarding organ donation: https://www.organdonor.gov/.

NOTES

1. Lawrence K. Altman, "New Homosexual Disorder Worries Health Officials," *The New York Times*, May 11, 1982, https://www.nytimes.com/1982/05/11/science/new-homosexual-disorder-worries-health-officials.html.

2. John Casey, "Dr. Fauci Calls Out Homophobic Lawmakers: 'The Antigay Attitude of People Is as Bad' As He's Ever Seen," *Advocate*, December 1, 2023, https://www.advocate.com/people/dr-fauci-homophobes-congress-hiv.

3. "What is Servant Leadership?" Robert K. Greenleaf Center for Servant Leadership, accessed May 1, 2024, https://www.greenleaf.org/what-is-servant-leadership/.

4. "Cardiovascular Disease is the No. 1 Killer of Women," Go Red for Women, accessed May 1, 2024, https://www.goredforwomen.org/en/.

5. Charlie Munger, "Charlie Munger: These 'Basic Rules' Made Me Successful in Life—'with Warren Buffett, I Had All 3,'" CNBC, December 20, 2023, https://www.cnbc.com/2023/11/29/charlie-munger-these-basic-career-rules-made-me-successful-in-life-with-warren-buffett-i-had-all-3.html.

6. Christine Bradstreet, "3 Quotes by Joseph Campbell That Will Encourage You to Follow Your Purpose," *Medium*, April 27, 2023, https://medium.com/ change-your-mind/3-quotes-by-joseph-campbell-that-will-encourage-you-to-follow-your-purpose-2b84e3be6c74.

7. "Organ Donor Statistics," Health Resources & Services Administration, reviewed March 2024, https://www.organdonor.gov/learn/organ-donation-statistics.

ABOUT THE AUTHOR

Throughout his 46-year career, John Stewart has served in diverse healthcare roles—including registration clerk, respiratory therapist, consultant, CEO, founder, and board member—in high-achieving Daughters of Charity organizations and health-tech startups. A proponent of putting physicians and patients at the core of healthcare, he continues to champion four key values: physician leadership development, servant leadership, data-driven process improvement, and supportive technology.

John began his career in healthcare as an ER registration clerk for Norton Children's Hospital in Louisville, Kentucky. His relationships there encouraged him to earn a bachelor's degree in respiratory therapy, which he leveraged when working in Norton Children's pediatric ICU, where he helped establish its first newborn ICU air transport team. These remarkable accomplishments led to his next role as assistant director of respiratory care within the newborn ICU at San Francisco Children's Hospital and firmly cemented John's dedication to quality patient care at all organizational levels.

He continued to serve in the healthcare industry as a consultant for Seton Medical Center, as the administrative director of the cardiac service line at O'Connor Hospital, as an administrator for the Heart and Vascular Institute at Sacred

Heart Health System, and as a senior consultant at Health Evolutions.

John then received the career-defining opportunity to work as the lead project consultant overseeing business plan development, strategic planning process, and construction of the Heart Center of Indiana. Accepting the role of CEO in 2004, his integration of core mission, vision, and values set the Heart Center on its course to achieving national recognition for quality and patient satisfaction as the largest cardiology group in the nation.

In 2010, as the president of the St. Vincent Medical Group in Indianapolis, he helped facilitate the organization's growth to over 1,200 providers across nearly 200 practice locations. Then, in August 2013, John played an integral part in the formation of Ascension Medical Group, one of the largest private healthcare systems in the United States with approximately 134,000 associates, 35,000 affiliated providers, and 140 hospitals across 19 states. As senior vice president, he and his team set into motion Athena, a common practice management platform and electronic health record system—an unprecedented initiative for its national scale. The project was completed an entire year ahead of schedule while still exceeding financial targets and transformed the physician enterprise's ability to deliver value-based, personalized care.

As of 2024, John serves on several boards, including Acesis, Inc., largely due to his advocacy for improved healthcare technology and data. Called to his passion for coaching and mentorship, he also serves as the founder of t4 Leadership Development & Consulting, helping leaders make innovative strides in healthcare.

In retirement, however, John looks forward to building more relationships in his now favorite city and home, Charleston, South Carolina; spending time with loved ones; traveling; writing; and caring for his English Cocker Spaniel, Bently.